Mamma used to say

PEARLS OF WISDOM FROM
THE WORLD OF YIDDISH

Mamma used to say

PEARLS OF WISDOM FROM THE WORLD OF YIDDISH

Rachel Sankevitz Rosmarin

TRANSLATED BY
Rabbi Yaakov Yosef Iskowitz

Feldheim Publishers
Jerusalem • New York

Originally published in 1997 in Hebrew
as *Peninim mi-Beis Ima* by Feldheim Publishers.

ISBN 1-58330-423-1
First published 2000
Copyright © 2000 by
Rachel Rosmarin and Feldheim Publishers

Designed by Chaim A. Cohen

All rights reserved. No part of this publication may be translated, reproduced, stored in a retrieval system or transmitted, in any form or by any means, electronic, mechanical, photocopying, recording, or otherwise, without permission in writing from the publishers.

FELDHEIM PUBLISHERS
POB 35002 / Jerusalem, Israel
200 Airport Executive Park, Nanuet, NY 10954
www.feldheim.com

Printed in Israel

Library of Congress Cataloging-in-Publication Data
Peninim mi-bet ima. English
　Mamma used to say : pearls of wisdom from the world of Yiddish / [compiled by] Rachel Rosmarin ; translated by Rabbi Yaakov Yosef Iskowitz.
　　p. cm.
　Proverbs in Yiddish, romanized Yiddish, and English, with translations and commentary in English.
　ISBN 1-58330-423-1 (hardcover)
　1. Proverbs, Yiddish. 2. Proverbs, Yiddish -- Translations into English. 3. Hasidic parables. I. Rozmarin, Rahel. II. Title.

PN6519.J5 P4613 2000
398.9'391--dc21   00-039303

❧ ACKNOWLEDGMENTS ☙

I am indebted to Mrs. Peninah Lichtenstein (the author A. Margalit), through whose encouragement, inspiration, and direction the book was created. I would also like to express my gratitude to:

Mrs. Chaya Kiel, who assisted me throughout the writing, editing, and designing of the book, all with excellent taste and expertise;

Rabbi Yaakov Yosef Iskowitz for his lucid translation from the Hebrew;

Mr. Chaim Cohen, of "Chen Advertising," for his advice and assistance, in both the planning and implementation of the design;

Mrs. Eva Hollander, for her sensitive editing of the manuscript;

The design, production, and editorial staff at Feldheim Publishers for their professional expertise.

Last but not least, I am grateful to my beloved family for their constant support, that has brought me this far.

May they be blessed from the Source of all blessings!

Rachel Rosmarin
Jerusalem
Adar II, 5760
March 2000

❧ CONTENTS ☙

In Remembrance, ix

About the Book, xi

How Goodly Are Your Tents, 1
The Jewish Home 3

I Have Been Young and Am Now Old, 23
From Youth to Old Age 25

What Is Man?, 37
A. Human Qualities 39
B. Differences between a Wise Person and a Fool 66

Interpersonal Relations, 77

Caring for the Needy, 107
A. The Character and Condition of the Poor, the Sick, and the Distressed 109
B. Support and Guidance to Those Who Perform Kindnesses 120

From Planning to Doing, 127
A. Planning and Performance, Will and Ability, Confronting and Overcoming 129
B. Work and the Professions 149

Every Word Counts, 155
A. Speech and Silence 157
B. Truth and Falsehood 163
C. Praises, Wishes, and Blessings 169
D. Encouraging Words for the Suffering and the Needy 173

A Time for Everything, 179
A. How Man Uses and Is Influenced by Time 181
B. The Symbolism of Festivals and Other Occasions 186

By the Sweat of Your Brow, 197
Money, Trade, and Livelihood 199

Perceiving God through Human Eyes, 219
The Creator's Eminence – Faith in Him and in Divine Providence 221

The Virtuous and Their Ways, 235
A. Advice and Guidance for Serving the Creator 237
B. Sincere Chasidic Devoutness 262
C. A Jew's Virtues 270

Of and About Reality, 275
About This and That 277

My Mother — In Loving Memory, 299

○₃ *IN REMEMBRANCE* ○○

My mother, Rebbetzin Chaya Freida Sankevitz, ע״ה, was born on 1 Elul 5660 (1900) and passed away on 27 Adar 5747 (1987). Hashem bestowed kindness on me during the days of mourning and introspection following her death, when He helped me recall, among the many other memories, the wonderful Yiddish sayings I had heard at home over the decades, sayings whose luster had not dimmed and whose flavor had remained as fresh as ever. Realizing the value of this treasure house, I hurried to collect them and put them into writing. Within a short period of time, I had gathered hundreds of these gems, sayings that my mother had used throughout her lifetime.

Mamma, ע״ה, would weave her epigrams into life's experiences and events. Thus was she able to convey objective lessons that were broad in scope, lessons that had the power to open one's eyes as well as one's heart.

Torah and greatness came together in her wisdom. She was the loyal wife of my beloved father and teacher, Rabbi Yaakov Chanoch Sankevitz, זצ״ל, the dean of Yeshivas Sefas Emes, and was the daughter of Rabbi Yehudah Leib Freibaum, הי״ד.

As we went through all the objects that had been in our parents' home, it seemed that everything was saturated with Mamma's words — words of wisdom that infused them with sweetness and charm, evoking in us the desire to embrace them with yearning.

Mamma used to preface her sayings with "Our Sages said"; "Tzaddikim used to say"; "It is written in the holy books"; "Back in Warsaw they would say"; or "Jewish grandmothers used to say"; etc. In so doing, she was describing herself as a mere messenger bringing exquisite old wine from an ancient winepress, words of wisdom from our venerable ancestors. She also used to say: "A Yiddish saying is, to a certain degree, like Torah." In other words: Jewish sayings have their source in the Torah and must be treated as such!

Many Jewish mothers, like my own, have throughout the ages wisely brought the Torah into their homes and daily lives, not only through the written word but even more so, by their heartfelt spoken words. These words penetrated their families' hearts and served as a guide to living Torah. Indeed, to commit to writing sayings that have been orally transmitted detracts from their flavor and special charm. R' Yitzchak of Vorki said, "A proverb's brilliance was not meant to be written down; its flash cannot be captured in writing."

Nevertheless, in order to preserve our mothers' Torah, we have with trembling hands put these sayings into writing, with a prayer that they fulfill the goal of "...and forsake not the teaching of your mother" (*Mishlei* 1:8).

Surely such words are rooted in sanctity, for our virtuous mothers lived only to fulfill God's will as set forth in His holy Torah, as interpreted and practiced by the Sages. We have therefore sought the holy origins of these sayings and have cited the sources, or what are believed to be the sources, from which they have been derived. Thus the reader can understand the depths of their true meaning.

The sources cited are not necessarily the oldest or the only ones. Sometimes they do not mean exactly what the saying does, but are used instead to explain or elaborate upon something that is connected to it, or to clarify a linguistic or other aspect.

Since the main goal of this collection is to teach important lessons, with the special flavor of Mamma's words, even to those who have never been exposed to such words, we have appended to each saying an explanation of its literal and/or metaphorical meaning, its lessons (where applicable), and its use.

ॐ *ABOUT THE BOOK* ॐ
by A. Margalit

We have all been raised on our mothers' prolific words of wisdom — words that embody the flash of a hinting wink, that are full of the nectar of life experience, that are succinctly phrased yet laden with meaning within — and, even more so, between — the lines.

During our childhood and youth, many of us grew up with such maxims, maxims that knew how to hit the mark every time, in every place, and in any situation. We made an everlasting acquisition of wise, well-turned phrases whose incisiveness spiced the routine, aroused our dormant senses, and soothed our wounds.

Mrs. Rachel Rosmarin, an educator and editor, has taken the concrete step of compiling this treasure-house of sayings and saving them from oblivion. Painstakingly, as a bee collects nectar from flowers, she began putting together the words of wisdom that her righteous mother would say to her family at every opportunity, in succulent and evocative Yiddish. Little by little, jolted out of the recesses of her memory, they were rescued from oblivion.

Once the effort was under way, it felt as if the words themselves were awakening from a long slumber to drag each other toward immortality. The glue of association pulled one after another out of the depths of time; it was as if a tremor had jolted the words from a deep sleep. The maxims and catch-phrases began streaming forth from the locked chambers of the past.

Deeply moved and with unbounded love, the author then began gathering these beloved and familiar pearls of wisdom. She classified them cautiously, as though carrying a precious load, and she translated them into Hebrew with great precision, taking great care to preserve their special flavor and not to deviate from their multilayered meanings.

She painstakingly researched the differences in linguistic nuances among the various versions, consulting Yiddishists and other experts, sparing neither effort nor resources to determine the correct usage.

Thus did *Mamma Used to Say* come into being. This unique work will serve not only as a beacon on the path of life, but also as a memorial to the author's mother, Rebbetzin Chaya Freida Sankevitz, ע"ה, a faithful mother in Israel, wife of the Gaon Rabbi Yaakov Chanoch Sankevitz, זצ"ל.

How instructive and exciting it is to browse through this book that is chock-full of hidden wisdom. It is imbued with love for the mother and wife who willingly left the comforts of the Diaspora to find refuge within the humble walls of the Holy City. It was there that her fountain of wisdom flourished, invigorating the souls of her children and her many acquaintances.

As you begin to read, contentment overtakes you. You read further and nod in enthusiastic agreement. How much wisdom is found in these words, how much of life's experience! Your eyes fill with tears — it is as if you have come back to your mother's home for a time. You sense that she is sharing with you, through wise sayings, her most cherished teachings, guiding, encouraging, and supporting you. You are transported back to the enchanting past, and in your heart, longing and yearning awaken and overflow. You thirstily imbibe of the good, old wine, whose taste and aroma have not deteriorated, but, on the contrary, continue to improve with age. This is because the wine has been brought to you from the best winery and blended from the world's choicest grapes: from your own mother's home.

This book is a loving tribute to a righteous wife and mother. For many of us, however, it also serves as a repository of our past, of our very roots. The wisdom in this book takes us back to the words: "Look to the rock from which you were hewn, to the quarry from which you were dug. Look back to Avraham your father and to Sarah who brought you forth" (*Yeshayahu* 51:1, 2).

We are greatly indebted to the author for granting us the enriching experience of reading this book. She has also more than earned our blessings for the special way in which she chose to honor her mother — by transmitting with awe and reverence the treasure of her wisdom. In the words of the Ramchal, "Fortunate is the person who has found wisdom and knowledge, who speaks to an attentive ear."

How Goodly Are Your Tents

HOW GOODLY ARE YOUR TENTS
THE JEWISH HOME

אַ ווײַב מאַכט פֿון דעם מאַן אַ נאַר אָדער אַ האַר.

A veib macht fun dem man a nar oder a har.

A wife can turn her husband into a master or a fool.

MEANING
A wife has great influence in shaping her husband's character.

IN THE SOURCES
The story is told of a pious couple who were childless. Believing that they were not adequately serving God in their present situation, they obtained a divorce. The pious man married a wicked woman who proceeded to corrupt him. The pious woman, however, married an evil man and made him righteous. This demonstrates the overriding influence of a wife.
(Bereshis Rabbah 17:7)

מיט אַ שלעכטע ווײַב אויף אַ יריד, און מיט קליינע קינדער אויף אַ חתונה

Mit a shlechte veib oif a yerid, un mit kleine kinder oif a chasseneh

With a bad wife at a fair, and with tiny tots at a wedding

METAPHORICAL MEANING
Describes situations where the presence of certain people is apt to be especially disruptive.

אַ מאַן מיט אַ װײַב זענען װי אַ איינס מיט אַ נול.

A man mit a veib zennen vie a eins mit a nul.

A married couple is like the combination "one and zero."

MEANING

Whereas "0" adds nothing when placed before "1," when it follows it multiplies by ten.

METAPHORICAL MEANING

A wife's contribution to the home is proportional to her ability to complement her husband: She contributes nothing by giving precedence to her opinion over his, but enhances his immensely by augmenting it!

אַ מאַמע דאַרף בעטן.

A mamme darf beten.

A mother should pray.

EXPLANATION

The Almighty surely answers the earnest, heartfelt prayers of a mother for her household. It is therefore appropriate that she pray intensely.

IN THE SOURCES

A cry is heard in Ramah, wailing, bitter weeping – Rachel weeping for her children. (Yirmeyahu 31:14)

Women are obligated to pray, despite the fact that prayer is a rabbinical time-related mitzvah, because prayer is an appeal for mercy, and women too are in need of mercy.
(Ramban, Sefer ha-Mitzvos, Aseh #5)

אַז מ'האָט קינדער אין די וויגן, דאַרף מען לאָזן לייטן צופרידן.

Az m'hot kinder in die viegen, darf men lozen leiten tzufrieden.

While your children are still in the cradle, let other people rest contented.

METAPHORICAL MEANING
As long as your own children are still young, and you haven't yet proven your ability and wisdom in raising and educating them, don't criticize other people's ways of rearing and teaching theirs.

IN THE SOURCES
Let one who girds his sword not boast like one who ungirds it. (Melachim I 20:11)

קינדער זענען ווי געלט אויף פּראָצענט.

Kinder zennen vie gelt oif protzent.

Children are like an interest-bearing investment.

METAPHORICAL MEANING
Investing one's efforts in raising and educating children yields ever-increasing results in all succeeding generations.

IN THE SOURCES
One of the six things of which man eats the fruits in this world, while the principal remains for him in the world to come: rearing one's sons to the study of Torah. (Shabbos 127a)

איז ער אַ גבר? – זאָל ער קרייען!

Iz er a gever? – Zol er kreien!

If he's a rooster, let him crow!

EXPLANATION
The Hebrew word "gever" has three meanings: man, hero, and rooster. The above aphorism is directed at all three.

METAPHORICAL MEANING
Let him prove his manhood by asserting himself!

IN THE SOURCES
King Solomon's friend implored the king to teach him the languages of birds and animals. The king agreed, but warned him: "You are asking me to divulge a great secret. Guard it very well, for on the day you reveal it you will surely die!"

After having acquired his new skills, the man returned home and began using them. One day he burst out laughing while listening to something funny "said" by his ox. His wife asked him what he was laughing about. His answer that it was a secret further aroused her curiosity, which was not dispelled even after he explained that if he told, he would die.

Giving in to her, the man assembled all his friends, parted from them and prepared himself to die after he would reveal his secret. Upon hearing of his master's impending death, the man's dog sat down in a corner of the yard and began howling. A sudden commotion at the other side of the yard caught the dog's attention: A rooster was strutting proudly, followed by a large bevy of hens and their chicks.

"Rooster, aren't you distressed by the terrible fate that awaits our master?" asked the dog.

"It's his fault for being so foolish," answered the rooster. "He has only one wife, and doesn't know how to treat her. Look, I have control over ten wives, none of whom dares to defy me, for they know that it would cause me to crow at them resoundingly!!!"

Upon hearing this, the man turned to his wife and said

firmly: "*Stop nagging me about my secret; if you don't, something terrible will happen to you!*"

His wife shuddered and never bothered him again. (Midrash)

איין קליינער קען מאַכן צוויי גרויסע צו ליגנערם.

Ein kleiner ken machen tzvei groisse tzu ligners.

One child can expose two adults as liars.

MEANING
A child who does not live up to his parents' praises of him undermines their credibility.

מיט קליינע קינדער קען מען נישט שטאָלצירן.

Mit kleine kinder ken men nisht shtoltziren.

One must not be boastful about little children.

MEANING
It is not advisable to brag about small children, because they are apt to change their behavior when in company.

IN THE SOURCES
May he increase our offspring and wealth like sand and like the stars at night.
(Zemiros l'Motza'ei Shabbos)

קינדער מיט געלט
איז אַ שיינע וועלט.

Kinder mit gelt iz a sheineh velt.

The world is beautiful when one has children and wealth.

MEANING
Parents who raise their children in comfort (and not in deprivation) can derive pleasure from them more readily.

שלאָף זיך אוים ביז די קליינע
קומען, טהו זיך אָן ביז די גרויסע
קומען.

Shlof zich ois biz die kleine kumen, tu zich on biz die groisse kumen.

Sleep well – until you have little children; dress well – until they grow up.

EXPLANATION
On little children, parents spend most of their time; on big ones, most of their money.

קליינע קינדער טראָגט מען אויף די הענט, גרויסע – אויפֿן קאָפּ.

Kleine kinder trogt men oif die hent, groisse – oif'n kop.

Small children are carried in one's arms; big ones – on the head.
(Little children, little troubles. Big children, big troubles.)

MEANING
Bringing up little children takes much physical effort; raising big ones taxes the spirit as well.

מ'וויינט און מ'וואַקסט.

M'veint un m'vakst.

One cries...and grows.

EXPLANATION
These words are used to console children having growing pains: they imply that the pains are what help them grow.

METAPHORICAL MEANING
An admonition: Some people "grow" – accomplish much in their various endeavors – but don't stop whining and complaining about their situation, no matter how successful they are.

WORDS OF OUR SAGES
Tears are the waste matter of the brain; the more a baby cries, the brighter it will be.
(Rabbi Pinchas of Koretz)

IN THE SOURCES

Rabban Gamliel married off his daughter. She beseeched him: "Father, please pray for me."

He responded: "I hope you don't come back here."

After giving birth to a son, she asked him again: "Father, please pray for me."

He answered: "I hope you won't stop saying 'Woe.'"

She said to him: "Father, why have you cursed me on my two joyful occasions?!"

Said he to her: "Both are prayers and blessings for you: May you live a good and peaceful life at home so that you will not have to return here; and in order that your son grow properly, that you do not stop saying 'Oy' – 'Oy, my son did not drink! Oy, my son did not eat! Oy, my son hasn't gone to shul!...'"

(Bereshis Rabbah 26:4)

דער "אוי" זאָל נישט אַרוים פֿון מויל.

Der "oy" zol nisht arois fun moil.

Don't stop saying "oy" (woe).

(Rabban Gamliel to his daughter)

EXPLANATION

This is a good wish, usually bestowed on a mother, that she should always be busy only with things that concern her children.

װאו אַ קינד פֿאַלט לײגט אַ מלאך אונטער אַ קישעלע.

Vu a kind falt leigt a malach unter a kisheleh.

When a child falls, an angel is there to place a cushion beneath him.

METAPHORICAL MEANING
God's great compassion accompanies a child's every step.

IN THE SOURCES
Hashem supports all who fall. (Tehillim 145:14)

Hashem protects the simple ["pesa'im"]. (Tehillim 116:6)

In the island cities a child is called "pesi." (Sanhedrin 110b)

דאָס ערשטע מײדל פֿירט דאָס רעדל.

Dos ershte meidel firt dos reidel.

The eldest daughter turns the wheel.

MEANING
As a daughter grows up, she helps her mother to properly care for and raise her younger siblings, who then learn from her example.

IN THE SOURCES
[If a] daughter [is born] first, it is a good sign for the children. (Bava Basra 141a)

IN THE SOURCES
A daughter is a vain treasure to her father: he has sleepless nights worrying about her. (Sanhedrin 100b)

אַ שטוב מיט טעכטער
איז גאָרנישט קיין געלעכטער!

A shtub mit techter iz gornisht kein gelechter!

A houseful of daughters is no joke!

MEANING
Raising daughters requires a father's serious commitment.

IN THE SOURCES
A father has compassion on his children, while their compassion is directed [not toward him but] to their [own] children. (Sotah 49a)

WORDS OF OUR SAGES
A father's devotion to his child is an inherited trait, handed down from Adam to his descendants. He could not pass on, however, a child's dedication to his father, since he himself had no father.
(R' Yechiel Michel of Ostrovtza)

איין טאַטע קען צען קינדער
אויסהאַלטן, און צען קינדער קענען
איין טאַטן נישט.

Ein tatteh ken tzen kinder ois'halten, un tzen kinder kennen ein tatten nisht.

One father can support ten children, but ten children can't support one father.
(R' Pinchas of Koretz)

MEANING
A father's instinctive dedication to his children is immeasurably greater than theirs to him.

How Goodly Are Your Tents

אַז דער טאַטע שענקט דעם זון, לאַכן ביידע; אַז דער זון שענקט דעם טאַטן, וויינען ביידע.

Az der tatteh shenkt dem zun, lachen beide; az der zun shenkt dem tatten, veinen beide.

When a father gives to his son, both laugh; when a son gives to his father, both cry.

MEANING
When a father gives to his son, the father is happy that his son has profited, and the son rejoices over the gift. When the son gives to the father, however, the latter cries out of humiliation, while the former bemoans his financial loss.

IN THE SOURCES
As a father has compassion upon [his] children.
(Tehillim 103:13)

דער טאַטע איז געטרײַ ווען די מאַמע איז דערבײַ.

Der tatteh iz getrei ven di mamme iz derbei.

A father dotes on his child as long as its mother is nearby.

MEANING
A father's feeling and expression of compassion for his child is in direct proportion to the mother's nearness.

IN THE SOURCES
As a mother comforts her son, so will I comfort you.
(Yeshayahu 66:13)

The mother, not the father, is mentioned because "a woman persuades by words more than a man does."
(Radak, based on Kiddushin 31a)

די ווינטערדיקע זון
איז ווי אַ שטיפמוטער.

Die vinterdikke zun iz vie a shtifmutter.

The winter sun is like a stepmother.

MEANING
The sun in winter is like a stepmother: no matter how radiant, its warmth is lacking.

אין אַ טשאָלנט און אין אַ שידוך
קוקט מען נישט צו פיל אַרײַן.

In a cholent un in a shidduch kukt men nisht tzu fiel arein.

Don't probe too deeply – into cholent, or when investigating a potential match.

EXPLANATION
Cholent, a Sabbath stew which is kept hot overnight, is comprised of various ingredients. Some lose their original taste and shape when mixed with others. It is futile, therefore, to investigate their true nature, since they are insignificant in relation to the dish's special taste. The saying makes use of the above fact to convey the following message about matchmaking: One ought to focus on clarifying that which is most important, and, when necessary, forgo delving into less salient points.

WORDS OF OUR SAGES

When looking for a match, it is impossible to find one that is completely perfect and only the best. It is also impossible to assess all possible outcomes. As long as its main elements are satisfactory, it might be best to yield when it comes to secondary matters that appear to be less so.

(Rabbi M. M. Schneerson of Lubavitch, Shaarei Halachah u-Minhag)

אַ שוויגער דאַרף פֿערמעגען פיר "ש": שלינגען, שוויַיגען, שמייכלען און שענקען.

A shvigger darf fermeggen fier "shin": shlingen, shveigen, shmeichlen un shenken.

A mother-in-law must adopt four [words that begin with] "s": swallow, silence, smile and spend.

MEANING

In order to have a good relationship with her daughter-in-law, a mother-in-law should adopt the following four tips, all of which begin with the letter "S." She should:

a. *swallow* – hold herself back from interfering in her son's family's life, no matter how tempting it may be to do so;

b. be *silent* – even when there is reason to react;

c. *smile* – always act graciously; and

d. *spend* – despite everything, continue to bestow kindness in every way.

מ'זאָגט די טאָכטער און מ'מיינט די שנור.

M'zogt die tochter un m'meint die shnur.

It's said to the daughter, but meant for the daughter-in-law.

MEANING

Some words are likely to harm the fragile relationship between a woman and her daughter-in-law. When necessary, she should say them to her daughter, intending them, however, for her daughter-in-law's ears.

METAPHORICAL MEANING

This applies to anyone who directs his words to one person with the intention that another get the message.

> **IN THE SOURCES**
> "[And Moses] was angry with Aaron's sons Eleazar and Ithamar" – Out of respect for Aaron, [Moses] turned his face to [Aaron's] sons and expressed his anger.
> (Rashi, quoting the Sifra to Vayikra 10:16)

אַ איידעם איז אַ שטיק שווער.

A eidem iz a shtik shver.

A son-in-law is a bit like his father-in-law.

MEANING

A man resembles his father-in-law in many ways.

> **IN THE SOURCES**
> A man's son-in-law is as his son. (Rashi to Shabbos 23b)

אַ באָבאַ דאַרף אַ פֿאַרטוך מיט גרױסע קעשענעס.

A bobbe darf a fartuch mit groisse keshenes.

A grandmother needs an apron with big pockets.

MEANING

Grandmothers have a strong desire to give things to their grandchildren, who, in turn, expect much from them. There is enormous benefit in such giving. That is why she needs big, stuffed pockets!

אַ מאַמע האָט גלעזערנע אױגן; אַ באָבע, מעשענע.

A mamme hot glezerneh oigen; a bobbe, mesheneh.

A mother's eyes are made of glass; a grandmother's, of brass.

MEANING

Mothers are very partial when appraising their children. Therefore, their eyes are as if made of glass: they seem to see, but don't. Grandmothers' eyes are even more prejudiced: their blindness (to grandchildren's faults) is apparent, as if they had brass eyes.

IN THE SOURCES
Would a father testify against his son?!
(Avodah Zarah 3b)

WORDS OF OUR SAGES
In the eyes of the wise, there is no greater fool than he. In his father's eyes, there is no one wiser than he.
(Rabbi Yehudah Alcharizi)

Since the day that Esau deceived his father Isaac, no one is able to see any evil in his son.
(Rabbi Israel Ba'al Shem Tov)

IN THE SOURCES

The crown of the aged are children's children, and the glory of children are their parents. (Mishlei 17:6)

When are parents the glory of their children? When children follow in their parents' footsteps. But if they do not, they are a disgrace and great liability to them, like a branch that renounces its roots.
(Rabbenu Bachya ad loc.)

דער זיידע איז אַ לייב,
דער טאַטע איז אַ בער;
דער עיקר, ווער איז ער?!

*Der zeide iz a leib, der tatteh iz a ber;
der ikker, ver iz er?!*

His grandfather is a lion, and his father, a bear; what is he ?!

METAPHORICAL MEANING
Noble ancestry is important, but only as an addendum to one's own "pedigree."

IN TALES OF THE CHASIDIM
A scion of holy parentage appeared before R' Shmuel Eliyahu of Zwolen. The latter asked him, "Who are you?" He answered: "The son of such-and-such Rebbe."

Said R' Shmuel: "You are from a distinguished family, but you have not told me who you yourself are. We pray, 'Our God and God of our forefathers,' which shows that our own reputation takes precedence."

*   *   *

R' Yisrael of Ruzhin used to tell the following:

A nobleman's dog had aged and could no longer accompany him on hunting trips. The nobleman could not bring himself to kill the dog, so he decided to get rid of it in another way: he wrapped it in lion and bear skins and sent it off into the forest.

The lion was then holding court, but observed that the animals were slipping away one by one.

Said the lion to the fox, "What's the special occasion?"

The fox checked things out and said, "A new king has arrived in the forest, a lion-bear!"

Filled with anxiety, the lion told the fox, "Go find out what kind of a king this is and report back to me."

The fox came and bowed before the new king and asked submissively, "Who are you, Sire?"

Answered the dog proudly, "My grandfather was a lion!"

The fox bowed again and asked, "And what are you?"

"My father was a bear!" answered the dog boldly.

The fox continued to probe, "Your father was a bear and your grandfather a lion, but, Sire, what are you?!"

"I...I am a dog."

The fox bowed mockingly and ran off to tell the lion.

בלוט איז נישט קיין וואַסער.

Blut iz nisht kein vasser.

Blood is not water.
(Blood is thicker than water.)

EXPLANATION
This is a metaphor that explains why people have feelings of kinship and dedication toward relatives.

IN THE SOURCES
Spill it [the blood of beasts and cattle] on the ground like water. (Devarim 12:16)

He who spills human blood shall have his own blood spilled by man. (Bereshis 9:6)

(We see that human blood is distinguished from that of animals, which is spilled like water. This distinction manifests itself in the quality of the relationship between human blood relatives.)

זכות אבות איז קיין קאַטאָוועס.

Z'chus ovos iz kein katovess.

Ancestral merits are no triviality.

MEANING
See IN THE SOURCES section.

IN TALES OF THE CHASIDIM
R' Simcha Bunim of Otwock was seventeen when his father, R' Mendel of Warka, died, and the Chasidim wished to appoint him in his father's place.

R' Simcha Bunim then took a trip to R' Yaakov Aryeh of Radzymin, one of the generation's elder Chasidic Rebbes, to ask for his support. He stood in line with the other Chasidim. When his turn came, the Rebbe of Radzymin said to him:

"We knew your grandfather, R' Yitzchak of Warka. We also heard about your father. And what now?"

The young scholar answered:

"Our forefather Abraham dug wells, and so did Isaac. We don't find that Jacob dug any, for since his ancestors had dug wells of 'living waters' it was easy for him to make use of them."

Upon hearing the answer, the Rebbe stretched out his hand and exclaimed, "Peace be unto you, Rebbe of Warka!"

IN THE SOURCES

Fortunate are the righteous! Not only do they acquire merit, but they bestow it upon their children and children's children to the end of all generations.
(Yoma 87a)

I [God] perform kindness for thousands [of generations] for those who love Me and keep My commandments.
(Shemos 20:6)

All Israel's successful endeavors are in the merit of that dust which Jacob raised [when wrestling with the angel].
(Shir ha-Shirim Rabbah 3)

As soon as Moses mentioned ancestral merit, Hashem said, "I have forgiven, as you requested."
(Devarim Rabbah 3)

In the days to come...I will skip [to redeem the Jews before the pre-determined] end in the merit of their forefathers.
(Tanchuma, Bemidbar 14)

אומעטום איז גוט, און בײַ זיך אין דער הײם איז נאָך בעסער.

Umetum iz gut, un bei zich in der heim iz noch besser.

Everywhere is fine, but home is even better.
("There's no place like home!")

MEANING
One's independence and privacy are guaranteed only at home.

IN THE SOURCES
Man is happy when he dwells in his own home.
(Yerushalmi Mo'ed Katan 2:4)

Each and every man is a king in his own home.
(Avos d'Rabbi Nasan 28:3)

וואויל איז דעם וואָס זיצט אין דער הײם.

Voil iz dem vos zitzt in der heim.

Happy is he who stays at home.
(Home is where the heart is.)

MEANING
Fortunate is he who merits to always stay in his own house, thereby enjoying all its advantages.

IN THE SOURCES
This is a play on the words, "Fortunate are they who dwell in Your house."
(Tehillim 84:5)

I Have Been Young and Am Now Old

I HAVE BEEN YOUNG AND AM NOW OLD
FROM YOUTH TO OLD AGE

אַזוי ווי מ'וויגט איינעם איַין אַזוי וויגט ער זיך אוים.

Azoy vi m'vigt einem ein azoy vigt er zich ois.

As a baby is rocked in the cradle, so will it move on through life.

MEANING
A person's development is influenced by the care he received as a baby and by the environment into which he was born.

IN THE SOURCES
He [Rabban Yochanan ben Zakkai] used to enumerate the merits of his disciples: ...Rabbi Yehoshua ben Chananyah, fortunate is she who bore him. (His mother used to bring his cradle to the house of study, to attune his ears to words of Torah from infancy. His teacher is here pointing out that his greatness was due to this act of hers.) (Avos 2:11)

Rabbi Chanina said: The warm baths and oil with which my mother anointed me in my youth have stood me in good stead in my old age. (Chullin 24b)

הונדערט און איינס איז אַלץ איינס.

Hundert un eins iz alts eins.

A hundred and one are both the same.

MEANING
The behavior of the very old can resemble that of a baby.

IN THE SOURCES

The...barley was destroyed [during the hailstorm], since the barley was ripe [was already in stalks]. But the wheat and spelt were not destroyed, since they ripen late [were still yielding – Rashi].
(Shemos 9:31, 32)

If the twig of a vine was not bent when it was young and moist, it will no longer be possible to bend it. Similarly, train a child when he is young.
(Midrash Mishlei 22:6)

אַ יונג ביימעלע בייגט זיך; אַ אַלטס ברעכט זיך.

A yung beimeleh beigt zich; a alts brecht zich.

A young tree bends; an old one breaks.

EXPLANATION
A young tree is pliable and bends from the force of the winds of a storm, but straightens up when it is over. An old tree, however, whose trunk has hardened with age, will break in the strong winds.

METAPHORICAL MEANING
A young person will easily adjust to the changing winds of life, whereas they may break an older person.

IN THE SOURCES

Do not cast me off in old age; when my strength fails, do not forsake me.
(Tehillim 71:9)

What is the meaning of "לעת מצוא" – "at a time of finding" or "beginning" – (Tehillim 32:6)? – when one encounters old age. A person must pray that in old age he will still be able to see, eat, and walk – for when one becomes old, everything abandons him.
(Tanchuma Miketz 10)

רבונו של עולם, דיך צו דינען, און זיך צו באדינען, מיטן גאנצען זינען.

Ribono shel olam, dich tzu dienen, un zich tzu badienen, mit'n gantzen zinnen.

Ribono shel olam, enable me to serve you of sound mind and to care for myself with honor.

MEANING
A petition of the elderly.

צו וואָס מ'געוויינט זיך אין דער יוגענט, בײַ דעם בלײַבט מען אויף דער עלטער.

Tzu vos m'geveint zich in der yugent, bei dem bleibt men oif der elter.

Even in old age one clings to habits acquired in youth, or: "Habits are hard to break."

AS INTERPRETED BY OUR SAGES
Desire, unlike physical strength, does not lessen with age, for although one grows weaker the force of habit becomes more ingrained.
(Rabbi Pinchas of Koretz)

IN THE SOURCES
Train a child according to his way; even when he grows old, he will not depart from it. (Mishlei 22:6)

[Some of our Sages used to say:] Fortunate is our youth that has not disgraced our old age. (Sukkah 53a)

WORDS OF OUR SAGES
As a monkey imitates people, an older person imitates himself by acting as he did when young. Therefore, "Train a child according to his way" – train him to work hard to perfect himself – and then, "even when he grows old, he will not depart from it," from his way. Rather, he will continue to train himself even when he is old.
(R' Menachem Mendel of Kotzk)

ווי איינער צו זיבן איז ער צו זיבעציק.

Vi einer tzu zibben iz er tzu zibetzik.

At seventy like at seven.

MEANING
A person's basic traits accompany him throughout life.

IN THE SOURCES
Even a youth is known by his behavior, whether his actions are pure and honest. (Mishlei 20:11)

Every pumpkin can be known [as soon as it begins to grow] from its stalk. (Berachos 48a)

WORDS OF OUR SAGES
All attributes that a person has in the prime of life or in old age were already there in his childhood and youth. (The Ways of the Righteous)

וואויל איז דעם וואָס פירט אויס בכבוד זיין וועלט.

Voil iz dem vos firt ois b'chavod zein velt.

Fortunate is he who completes his days with honor.

MEANING
See IN THE SOURCES section.

IN THE SOURCES
Fortunate is he who was raised in the Torah; whose toil was in the Torah; who has given pleasure to his Creator; who grew up with a good name and departed the world with a good name. (Berachos 17a)

וואויל איז דעם קייזער וואָס ווערט באַגליקט אויף די עלטערע יאָרן.

Voil iz dem keizer vos vert baglikt oif die eltereh yoren.

Fortunate is the emperor who attains happiness in old age.

IN THE SOURCES
The end of a matter is better than its beginning.
(Koheles 7:8)

Hashem blessed the latter years of Iyov's life more than the former...and Iyov died old and contented.
(Iyov 42:12-17)

EXPLANATION
Said upon hearing of someone's late success: Happy is he who has the good fortune to end his days on earth in bliss (although it may have previously eluded him).

IN TALES OF THE CHASIDIM
When R' Nachum of Slonim learned that when Rabbi Akiva was teaching he recalled the deeds of his youth *(Avos d'Rabbi Nasan 21)*, he thought there would follow a description of Rabbi Akiva's remorse over his wasted years.

To his surprise, however, the story continued on to describe Rabbi Akiva's joy and thanks to the Almighy for his later good fortune: He said: "I thank You, Hashem, my God, for setting my portion with those who sit in the House of Study."

This greatly surprised R' Nachum, who said: "Let us learn from this not to grieve over times gone by, but rather to raise our spirits with gladness and thanks to Hashem for the good we finally attained."

IN THE SOURCES

David said: Master of the Universe, Man constantly aspires to a better condition: If he is poor, he wants to be rich; if he is weak, he hopes to become strong; if he is sick, he wishes to be well. But there is no hoping to be saved from death.
(Tanchuma, Berachah, 6)

אַז מען לעבט, דערלעבט מען.

Az men lebt, derlebt men.

Only by living may one overcome.
(One has to "roll with the punches.")

MEANING
Words of encouragement to one who has always struggled through adversity to finally find happiness in old age: Confronting life's challenges enables one to attain peace and contentment.

IN THE SOURCES

As long as a person is alive, there is hope; once he dies, his hope is no more.
(Yerushalmi, Berachos 9:1)

Even if a sharp sword rests on a man's neck, let him not desist from [praying for] mercy. (Berachos 10a)

Hope to Hashem.
(Tehillim 27:14)

ווי לאַנג די אויגן זענען אָפֿן דאַרף אַ מענטש האָפֿן.

Vie lang die oigen zennen offen, darf a mentsh hoffen.

Where there's life, there's hope.
(Hope springs eternal. Lit., a play on words: As long as one's eyes are open ["offen"], one must hope ["hoffen"]).

אויף דער עלטער, אז מ'קען נישט גיין, לויפט מען.

Oif der elter, az m'ken nisht gein, loift men.

In old age, when one can no longer walk, one runs.

MEANING

The saying uses a paradox, apparently, to draw attention to a common feeling among the elderly: that life is slipping away, which drives them to accelerated activity despite their limitations. ("You should live till you die.")

IN THE SOURCES

Repent a day before you die.
(Avos 2:15)

Happy is our old age which has atoned for our youth.
(Sukkah 53a)

די גרויסע קײַען, די קליינע שפּײַען.

Die groisse keien, die kleine shpeien.

Adults chew, children spew.

MEANING

Children divulge with their words that which adults are in the habit of doing.

IN THE SOURCES

Abbaye said: Yes, as the saying goes, "The talk of a child in the marketplace is that of either its father or mother." Rashi: A common proverb meaning that whatever a child says in the marketplace, he heard from his father or mother.
(Sukkah 56b)

IN THE SOURCES
Thus people say: Many old camels are laden [saddled] with the hides of younger ones [that already died].
(Sanhedrin 52a)

נישט פון דער יוגענט לעבט מען,
און נישט פון דער עלטער שטאַרבט מען.

Nisht fun der yugent lebt men, un nisht fun der elter shtarbt men.

One does not live because of youth; nor does one die of old age.

MEANING
The laws of nature do not determine who will live or die. Every creature's life span is determined by God and is one of the mysteries of the world.

IN THE SOURCES
Against your will you live, against your will you die, and against your will you will give an account, etc.
(Avos 4:30)

נישט פון קיין נחת לעבט מען,
און נישט פון צרות שטאַרבט מען.

Nisht fun kein nachas lebt men, un nisht fun tzoros shtarbt men.

One does not live because of pleasure; nor does one die of distress.

MEANING
Desiring life does not guarantee it; neither does wishing to die (God forbid!) bring death. Indeed, our wishes are sometimes contradicted by reality. Life and death are dependent on Hashem's will alone!

אַז מ'דערמאַנט זיך אין טויט איז מ'נישט זיכער מיטן לעבן.

Az m'dermant zich in toit, iz m'nisht zicher mit'n leben.

Reminding oneself of death undermines one's trust in life.

MEANING

Man would like to behave as if he'll go on living forever: he tends to repress the fact that death is inevitable. Confronting death shakes his trust in life and reminds him that any day might be his last; accordingly, he must utilize it to the fullest. The saying may also be used ironically to mean that when one is reminded of someone who has already succumbed to death, he is no longer sure that he himself is actually still alive.

IN THE SOURCES
It is better to go to a house of mourning than to a house of feasting, for that is the end of...man, and the living should take it to heart. (Koheles 7:2)

אַ יונגער קען, אַ אַלטער מוז.

A yunger ken, a alter muz.

A youth might, an old person must.

MEANING

An expression of resigning oneself to the fact that old age terminates in death:
Death may strike the young; it definitely strikes the old.

IN THE SOURCES
The end of man is to die. (Berachos 17a)

WORDS OF OUR SAGES
Death is life's shore; old age is the boat that brings one to the shore...
(R' Avraham Chasdai)

אַן אַלטן מענטש קומט קיין טויט שטראָף נישט.

An alten mentsh kumt kein toit shtrof nisht.

An elderly person is not liable to the death penalty.

MEANING
Expression used when acceptance is the reaction to an elderly person's passing.

> **WORDS OF OUR SAGES**
> When an elderly person dies, people nod, as if to say, "Well, he was old." I don't comprehend: Are the elderly condemned to death? *(R' Ber of Ostrovtza)*

אַז מ'לעבט מיט רעכענונג, שטאַרבט מען מיט ווידוי.

Az m'lebt mit rechenung, shtarbt men mit viduy.

One who lives with a ledger dies with a confession.

MEANING
One must keep an ongoing account of his deeds, in order to confess them when repenting before death.

> **IN THE SOURCES**
> Let your garments always be white. *(Koheles 9:8)*
>
> Repent a day before you die. *(Avos 2:10)*

אַז מ'בעט זיך גוט דאָ,
ליגט מען גוט דאָרט.

Az m'bet zich gut doh, ligt men gut dort.

He who prepares his bed here will lie comfortably there.

METAPHORICAL MEANING
The reward in the world-to-come will be commensurate with our efforts in this world.

IN THE SOURCES
You accumulate Torah and mitzvos in this world, and I will store up reward for you in the world-to-come.
(Devarim Rabbah 7:10)

It is told about King Munbaz that he expended all his treasure and that of his fathers in years of scarcity. His brothers and his father's household came and said to him, "Your ancestors saved and added to the treasures of their fathers, and you are squandering them?!" He replied: "My ancestors hoarded below and I am storing above...they stashed where it can be tampered with, and I store where it cannot be tampered with...they put away that which produces no fruit, but I store something that does produce fruit...they saved money, but I am storing treasures of souls...they gathered for others, and I have gathered for myself... they hoarded for this world, but I am accumulating for the world-to-come. (Bava Basra 11a)

What Is Man?

WHAT IS MAN?

A. HUMAN QUALITIES

אַ מענטש איז שטאַרקער פיל מאָל פון אײַזן און פון שטאָל.

A mentsh iz shtarker fil mol fun eizen un fun shtol.

Humans are much stronger than iron or steel.

MEANING
Though composed of flesh and blood, man's spiritual powers make him much more durable than nature's strongest elements.

א אײַנרעדעניש איז ערגער ווי אַ קרענק.

A einredenish iz erger vi a krenk.

Self-delusion is worse than an illness.

MEANING
It is dangerous to cling to one's imagination and illusions, because one acting in such a manner is not perceived as being ill; therefore, no effort is made to heal him as is done when an illness *is* recognized.

IN THE SOURCES

Ten strong things were created in the world (in ascending order): ...iron is hard...the body is strong...
(Bava Basra 10a)

The plans in a man's heart are deep waters.
(Mishlei 20:5)

Every Jew has hidden powers of which even he is unaware.
(Imrei Emes, Vayigash)

WORDS OF OUR SAGES

Mental illness is worse than physical illness.
(R' Shem Tov of Falaquera)

IN THE SOURCES
If you find honey, eat only what you need, lest you stuff yourself and regurgitate it. (Mishlei 25:16)

WORDS OF OUR SAGES
Famine and hunger are spices for any dish.
(Rabbi Moshe Chefetz)

אַז דאָס מויל איז זאַט,
איז דאָס מעל ביטער.

Az dos moil iz zat, iz dos mehl bitter.

When the mouth is full, flour tastes sour.

MEANING
Eating when full makes one apt to criticize his food, or, Eating when full ruins the food's taste.

METAPHORICAL MEANING
Overindulgence in the pleasures of this world leads to a distaste for them.

WORDS OF OUR SAGES
Trying to run away from one's problems is like a woman in labor running off to another room...
(R' Yisrael Ba'al Shem Tov)

אַ מענטש קען פֿון זיך
נישט אַנטלויפֿן.

A mentsh ken fun zich nisht antloifen.

A person cannot run away from himself.

MEANING
One can't run away from his own identity and problems; he must cope with them.

What Is Man?

אַ מענטש איז זיך דער גרעסטער שונא.

A mentsh iz zich der grester sonei.

A person is liable to be his own worst enemy.

MEANING
It is in man's power to hurt and cause more harm to himself than his enemies can.

וואָס עס ווילט זיך, דאָס גלייבט זיך.

Vos es vilt zich, dos gleibt zich.

People believe what they want to.

MEANING
One tends to believe that only what he likes has happened, is happening , or will happen; he finds it hard to believe when things don't turn out that way.

ALTERNATIVE TRANSLATION

Partiality shapes one's beliefs.

MEANING
Our ideology is shaped by our desires and aspirations.

IN THE SOURCES
[Israel] engaged in idolatry only that they might openly satisfy their forbidden lusts.
(Sanhedrin 63b)

IN THE SOURCES

A man is shown in a dream only what is suggested by his own thoughts.
(Berachos 55b)

WORDS OF OUR SAGES

People are recognizable by their dreams; each according to his particular dream. In his dream, our forefather Jacob beheld "a ladder whose top reached heavenward... and Hashem was standing over him." Pharaoh, however, dreamt of "seven handsome cows...."
(R' Meir of Przemyslany)

Dreams enable us to recall what our mind was engrossed in all day.
(R' Simchah Bunim of Przysucha)

פֿון װאָס חלומט אַ גאַנז? פֿון האָבער!

Fun vos cholemt a ganz? Fun hober!

What does a goose dream about? Oats!

METAPHORICAL MEANING

One's personality and circumstances are reflected in his dreams and wishes.

IN TALES OF THE CHASIDIM

Once, at the end of Yom Kippur, R' Shlomo of Bobov asked a youth who had just finished praying in the Rebbe's Beis Midrash: "Tell me, what did you yearn for during the prayers?"

The simple lad answered innocently: "I was waiting for and looking forward to nightfall, so that I could eat already."

"Really?" said the Rebbe to him, "You were longing for nightfall, while we were fervently praying for the morning, for the dawning of the light of Mashiach."

עס איז בעסער אַ סך דאגות װי איין דאגה.

Es iz besser a sach deiges vi ein deigeh.

Better many worries than one.

MEANING

It is better to have many little worries in one's heart rather than to fill it with one big worry.

ער איז צו גאָט און צו לײַט.

Er iz tzu Gott un tzu leit.

He is good to God and good to man.

MEANING
This is a description of someone who is outstanding in his relationship to Hashem as well as in his dealings with other people.

IN THE SOURCES
And find favor and high regard in the eyes of God and man. (Mishlei 3:4)

He who is good to Heaven and good to man is a righteous man who is good. (Kiddushin 40a)

אַז מ'בעט אַ פּאַרך צום מנין, האַלט ער זיך אין גרויסן.

Az m'bet a parch tzum minyan, halt er zich in groissen.

Inviting a boor to complete a minyan raises his self-importance.

METAPHORICAL MEANING
One's self-image tends to be influenced by others' attitudes toward him.

IN THE SOURCES
Bil'am replied..."Balak, son of Tzippor, king of Mo'av, has sent me a message." (Bemidbar 22:10) – He became proud and said..."Kings are asking for me...." (Midrash Rabbah ad loc. 20:9)

"What is more," said Haman, "Queen Esther gave a feast, and besides the king she did not have anyone but me. And tomorrow too I am invited by her along with the king." (Esther 5:12) – Said Haman: "The king promotes me, his wife honors me, and there is no one greater than I in the entire kingdom," and he became very self-satisfied. (Midrash Rabbah ad loc. 9:2)

אַז דער רב טוט אַ שידוך מיטן
בעדער, האַלט זיך דער בעדער
פאַר אַ רב.

Az der rov tut a shidduch mit'n beder, halt zich der beder far a rov.

When the bath-house attendant makes a match with the rabbi, he feels he is as important as the rabbi.

MEANING
See previous saying.

IN THE SOURCES
No man leaves the world with even half his cravings fulfilled; if he has a hundred, he wants two hundred.
(Koheles Rabbah 1:34)

וואָס מ'האָט וויל מען נישט,
און וואָס מ'וויל האָט מען נישט.

Vos m'hot vil men nisht, un vos m'vil hot men nisht.

What we have we don't want, and what we want we don't have.

MEANING
There is a gap between the desirable and the available.

What Is Man?

וואַרפט אַרויס דעם אָרעמאַן; איך קען זײַן קרעכץ נישט פֿאַרנעמען.

Varft arois dem oremann; ich ken zein krechts nisht farnemen.

Throw the beggar out; I can't take his sighing.

METAPHORICAL MEANING
Reaction of a "refined person" who hides his responsibility toward people in distress behind the mask of hypersensitivity.

IN THE SOURCES
He who closes his ears to the cry of a poor man...
(Mishlei 21:13)

חן גייט איבער שיין.

Chein geit iber shein.

Grace is better than beauty.

MEANING
Grace is the reflection of the soul; hence it is better than physical beauty.

IN THE SOURCES
And [Esther] by her grace won his favor more than all the [other] maidens.
(Esther 2:17) – *Esther was of greenish complexion, but she was endowed with a touch of grace.* (Megillah 13a)

Every man who is endowed with grace is without doubt a God-fearing man.
(Sukkah 49b)

IN THE SOURCES
"All of man's toil is for his mouth, yet his desires are never satisfied." – He works his whole life for his mouth, but his soul does not become satisfied by his attainments.
(Seforno to Koheles 6:7)

WORDS OF OUR SAGES
The soul consoles and supports the aching body. However, when the soul is pained and full of worry, the body cannot console it.
(Rabbeinu Yonah)

מ'עסט נישט מיט קיין צען מיילער.

M'est nisht mit kein tzen meiler.

You can't eat with ten spoons (lit., "mouths").

METAPHORICAL MEANING
Criticism of people who are hurrying to get rich or to satisfy another desire. Man's appetite is greater than his physical needs and prevents him from becoming satisfied by meeting his real needs.

געלט פֿאַרלוירן נישט פֿאַרלוירן,
קרעדיט פֿאַרלוירן האַלב פֿאַרלוירן,
מוט פֿאַרלוירן אַלץ פֿאַרלוירן.

Gelt farloiren nisht farloiren; kredit farloiren halb farloiren; mut farloiren altz farloiren.

Money lost, nothing lost; credit lost, half lost; courage lost, everything lost.

MEANING
If you lose money, it is possible to continue functioning without it. Similarly, it is possible, though difficult, to restore creditability that has become tarnished. However, when one loses courage and the strength to cope – the foundation stones of all achievement and activity – nothing remains.

מ'געראָט נאָך דעם נאָמען.

M'gerot noch dem nommen.

One's name is instrumental in one's growth and development.

EXPLANATION
"Gerot" means both "succeed" and "similar." The proverb implies both meanings.
a. One's name alludes to one's personality and success in life.
b. There is a connection, and sometimes a similarity, between a person and the one for whom he was named.

IN THE SOURCES
Rabban Shimon ben Gamliel says: Our ancestors, through their divine inspiration, named their children according to [future] events. We, who are not divinely inspired, give them the names of our [righteous] forebears. (As their names were instrumental in their successful lives, so may they be for our children.) (Bereshis Rabbah 58, 37:7)

A person must always be careful in considering which name to give to his son, for it can serve as a good or an evil influence, as we find concerning the spies. (Tanchuma Ha'azinu 7)

There are some people of whom it is said that all who are called by their name will attain greatness, and that is what is meant by (Bereshis 48:16), "and may my name [Jacob] and the names of my forefathers [Abraham and Isaac] be called upon them." (Sefer Chasidim 244)

אייגנס איז ליב.

Eigens iz lieb.

One cherishes one's own.

MEANING

"A man is his own relative" *(Yevamos 25b)*, that is, he is partial to himself and to anything that is his.

IN TALES OF THE CHASIDIM

It happened once, that at the house of R' Yehudah of Lipsk, a child fell off the roof. The child's screams frightened the tzaddik terribly. Quickly he was told that the child was not one of his own. The Rebbe calmed down somewhat, but shortly burst into tears. "Is this how I love my fellow Jew, trembling over my own child and calming down when it's someone else's?! – I will not have attained true love of my fellow Jew until every single one of them is as close to my heart as my own son!"

> **IN THE SOURCES**
> A man prefers a kav [small measure] of his own to nine of his neighbor's.
> *(Bava Metzi'a 38a)*

וויינען און לאַכן זענען בײַ ווײַבער לייכטע זאַכן.

Veinen un lachen zennen bei veiber leichte zachen.

Women cry and laugh easily.

MEANING

Women are endowed with great sensitivity and are very emotional.

> **IN THE SOURCES**
> [A woman's] tears are frequent. *(Bava Metzi'a 59a)*

What Is Man?

די זאָרגט אַז די פּערל זענען איר צו שיטער, און די זאָרגט אַז די פּערלגריץ איז איר צו שיטער.

Die zorgt az die perl zenen ir tzu shitter, un die zorgt az die perlgritz iz ir tzu shitter.

This one worries that the pearls in her necklace are too small, and that one worries that the pearl barley in her soup is too meager.

MEANING
This is a criticism of people who worry about smallness: Women always worry; some worry unnecessarily about not being rich enough, whereas others worry understandably about being too poor.

WORDS OF OUR SAGES
Poorest is he whose heart aches from his poverty.
(Rabban Shimon ben Gamliel, Mivchar Ha-Peninim)

די אויגן זענען גרעסער פֿון דעם מויל.

Di oigen zenen gresser fun dem moil.

One's eyes are bigger than one's mouth.

METAPHORICAL MEANING
It is harder to satisfy the eyes than the mouth, because man's appetite is greater than his ability to derive joy from it.

IN THE SOURCES
The eye never has enough of seeing. (Koheles 1:8)

...nor can the eyes of man be satisfied. (Mishlei 27:20)

ער איז אַ "זייט מיר מוחל" מענטש.

Er iz a "zeit mir moichel" mentsh.

His entire personality says "please forgive me."

MEANINGS
a. This describes someone who constantly begs people's forgiveness. He seems polite and courteous, but his intentions are that people get out of his way because he is disgusted by them.
b. Criticism of someone who uses courteous words to excuse himself from helping others.

וואָס בײַ אַ ניכטערן אויף דער לונג איז בײַ אַ שִׁיכּורן אויף דער צונג.

*Vos bei a nichtern oif der lung
iz bei a shikkern oif der tzung.*

What soberness conceals, drunkenness reveals.

METAPHORICAL MEANING
With the loss of self-control, hidden truths are revealed.

IN THE SOURCES

In wine, out secret! When wine goes in, counsel departs. (Eruvin 65a)

A drunkard utters obscenities without shame. (Bemidbar Rabbah 10:6)

מ'קען נישט אַרויפֿזעצן אַ פֿרישן קאָפֿ.

M'ken nisht aroifsetzen a frishen kop.

I can't give him a new head.

METAPHORICAL MEANING

An expression accepting the fact that someone's way of thinking is inferior; it is impossible to change one's thinking process.

קיינער זעט נישט זײַן אייגענעם הויקער.

Keiner zet nisht zein eigenem hoiker.

We are blind to our own defects.

MEANING

A person is partial to himself. He is therefore biased when judging his own personality and has trouble discerning his character flaws.

IN THE SOURCES

One sees the blemishes of others but not one's own. (Nega'im 2:5; similarly, in Bechoros 38b)

A man cannot see [anything] to his own disadvantage. (Shabbos 119a)

IN THE SOURCES

The heart alone knows its bitterness. (Mishlei 14:10)

If the patient says, "I need it," while the physician says, "He does not need it," we listen to the patient. (Yoma 83a)

פרעג נישט דעם דוקטער, פרעג בעסער דעם קראַנקן.

Freg nisht dem doktor, freg besser dem kranken.

Better to ask the patient than the doctor.

MEANING
The patient will give a better description of his condition, based on his feelings, than the doctor, who will base it on his knowledge.

METAPHORICAL MEANING
He who suffers knows his condition better than those who are supposed to know it.

אַ אידענע האָט נייַן און נייַנציק נשמות.

A Iddeneh hot nein un neintzik neshomess.

A Jewish woman has ninety-nine souls.

METAPHORICAL MEANING
A Jewish woman's life is burdened to the point of exhaustion. Sometimes it looks as if she will collapse, but she soon recovers and appears to be infused with a new spirit.

אַ זאַטער קען דעם הונגעריקן נישט פֿאַרשטיין.

A zatter ken dem hungeriken nisht farshtein.

A sated person cannot understand a hungry one.

MEANING

A person who is well-off cannot understand the distress of one who is in misery.

IN TALES OF THE CHASIDIM

It was a cold winter night. A torrential rain was falling. The rabbi of Lodz, R' Eliyahu Chaim Meisel, was trekking through the mud among the houses of the generous, raising money to warm the poor, freezing townsfolk.

A servant met him at the door of the aristocrat Posnansky and invited him in. The rabbi remained at the doorway, however, and stubbornly resisted all efforts to have him enter the well-heated house. Having no alternative, the rich host, wearing a thin robe, was forced to leave his comfortable seat near the fireplace to talk to the rabbi near the open door. As if inadvertently, the rabbi slowly steered his host outside. After the cold had penetrated the aristocrat's body, the rabbi put forward his request and in fact received a generous contribution.

Finally, the host dared to ask, "Why did the rabbi refuse to enter my warm home?"

R' Eliyahu Chaim answered, "True, it is very cold out here, but if you hadn't stood outside yourself, you would never have been able to understand the suffering of the poor."

IN THE SOURCES

Do not judge your fellow until you have reached his place. (Avos 2:5)

He who is situated in a dark place sees what's in the light, but he who is in a lighted place cannot see what's in the dark.
(Tanchuma Tetzaveh)

WORDS OF OUR SAGES

The sated will not sense the pain of the starving.
(R' Shem Tov of Falaquera, Iggeres Ha-Mussar)

Don't share your sorrow with him who has none.
(Rabbi Shmuel Ha-Naggid)

ער קומט נישט אָן צו זיין פּאָדעשווע.

Er kumt nisht on tzu zein podeshveh.

He doesn't come up to his ankles.

METAPHORICAL MEANING
He is notably inferior (in knowledge, wisdom, wealth, etc.) to so-and-so.

> **IN THE SOURCES**
> *When Moses wanted to kill Og, King of Bashan, he took an ax ten cubits long, leapt ten cubits into the air, and only reached his ankle.*
> (Based on Berachos 54b)

דער קאָפּ טראָגט די פֿיס.

Der kop trogt di fis.

The head carries the feet.

METAPHORICAL MEANINGS
a. Describes a person who deliberates before taking action.
b. Describes one whose desire, or awareness of a necessity, drives him onward, although he may be physically spent.

> **IN THE SOURCES**
> *The body follows the head.*
> (Eruvin 41a)

אַ לעבעדיקער מענטש דאַרף.

A lebedikker mentsh darf.

A living person has needs.

MEANING
We must not disregard man's existential needs; they must be met to enable him to pursue and attain life's goals.

אַ שיקסע בײַ אַ רב קען אויך פּסקנען שאלות.

A shikseh bei a rov ken oich paskenen sheiles.

Experience is the best teacher. (Lit., "In the rabbi's home, even the non-Jewish maid can decide halachic questions.")

METAPHORICAL MEANING
One learns from his environment, even without trying.

IN THE SOURCES
Rabbi Shimon said: Tavi, the slave of Rabban Gamliel used to sleep under the bed [in the Sukkah], and Rabban Gamliel said to the Sages, "You have seen Tavi my slave, who is a scholar, and knows that slaves are exempt from [laws of] the Sukkah. That is why he sleeps under the bed."
(Sukkah 20b)

אַז מ'פרעגט אַ שאלה, איז "טרייף."

Az m'fregt a sheileh, iz "treif."

If you ask [the rabbi] a question, he'll find something wrong (lit., "not kosher").

EXPLANATION
Ignorant people would rather not pose questions of Kashrus to their rabbi, assuming that he will always pronounce the food not kosher.

METAPHORICAL MEANING
One must not put himself into situations where doubts as to the proper course of action arise.

IN THE SOURCES

"I will take you out from under the burdens [סבלות] of Egypt" – (from the סבלנות [patience] you show toward the Egyptians, by making the exile detestable in your eyes). The worst thing about Israel's exile in Egypt was that they no longer felt they were in exile!
(Chiddushei Ha-Rim to Shemos 6:6)

דער װאָרעם אין כרײן, מײנט אַז ס'איז נישטאָ בעסערס.

Der vorem in chrein meint az s'iz nishto bessers.

As blissful as a worm in horseradish (Ignorance is bliss.)

METAPHORICAL MEANING

Adaptation to a situation desensitizes one to its disadvantages.

אַ שטילער װאָרעם און גראָבט טיף

A shtiller vorem un grobt tif

A quiet worm that digs deep

METAPHORICAL MEANINGS

a. Describes a person who works quietly, almost undetectably, yet succeeds and reaches his goals.
b. Describes an apparently innocent person who is secretly subversive.

וואָס איינער האָט אין זיך וואַרפט ער פון זיך.

Vos einer hot in zich varft er fun zich.

Man exudes that which is in him. (Or: He has a blind spot about himself.)

METAPHORICAL MEANING
Man's relationship to his environment is affected by his character.

ער האָט אַ קאָפּ אויפן קאַרק.

Er hot a kop oifen kark.

He has a head on his shoulders (lit., neck).

METAPHORICAL MEANING
Description of one whose speech and actions attest to his being astute and of a firm and resolute mind.

IN THE SOURCES

He who declares others unfit is himself unfit, and stigmatizes others with his own blemish. (Kiddushin 70b)

The purity of one's thoughts may be determined from his lips. (Zohar)

WORDS OF OUR SAGES

One may see all blemishes except [lit., outside of] one's own. (Nega'im 2:5) – All blemishes that one sees outside himself, around him, derive from his own blemishes; it should alert him to the fact that he too has them.
(R' Yisrael Ba'al Shem Tov)

יעדער בעל-דרשן דרשנט פאַר זיך.

Yeder ba'al-darshen darshent far zich.

Every preacher preaches to himself.

MEANING

Preachers sermonize about things that concern themselves.

METAPHORICAL MEANING

Criticism directed at one who pretends to care about the concerns of the public while actually attending to his own.

> **IN THE SOURCES**
> He teaches merely for his own honor. *(Kiddushin 31a)*

די אייער ווילן זיַין קליגער פון די הינער.

Di eier villen zein kliger fun di hinner.

Eggs want to be wiser than hens.

METAPHORICAL MEANINGS

a. Normally, parents are superior to children until the latter mature. Accordingly, the maxim may be stated as a question: Can children purport to understand more than their elders?!

b. Sometimes children are greater and brighter than their parents. The saying, then, states a fact: Young people strive to – and can – become wiser than their elders.

> **IN THE SOURCES**
> Your own offspring teaches you reason! *(Yevamos 63a)*
>
> The son's power is more extensive than the father's. *(Shevu'os 48a)*

אַז מ'ברית זיך אָפּ מיט הייסן
בלאָזט מען אויפן קאַלטן.

Az m'brit zich op mit heissen blozt men oifen kalten.

Once bitten, twice shy.
(Lit., "Once burned by hot water, you'll blow even on cold.")
(We learn from bitter experience.)

METAPHORICAL MEANING
The bitter taste of failure causes extra wariness.

IN THE SOURCES
One who has been bitten by a snake will be frightened by a rope. (Koheles Rabbah 1)

אַ תם, און שטויסט ווי אַ מועד.

A tam, un shtoist vi a mu'ad.

An innocent ox, but it gores like one who gores habitually.
(Don't be fooled by appearances.)

METAPHORICAL MEANING
Description of a person who appears to be benign but is really brutish.

IN THE SOURCES
A "Tam" is an ox that has gored once or twice; a "Mu'ad" has gored three times and has to be killed. (Based on Shemos 21:28, 29)

IN THE SOURCES

Pinchas, son of Elazar...turned My anger away from the Israelites by zealously taking up My cause among them. (Bemidbar 25:11)

Pinchas saw...and rose up from the midst of the assemblage and took a spear in his hand. (Bemidbar 25:7)

IN THE SOURCES

Samson went down to Timnah...a full-grown lion came roaring at him...he tore him asunder as one might tear a kid...his strength slipped away from him...the Philistines seized him and gouged out his eyes.... (Shoftim 14–16)

פֿון פּנחס'ס עולם

Fun Pinchos's oilem

Of Pinchas's crowd
(He stands out in a crowd.)

MEANINGS

a. Critical remark about one who holds extremist views; one who is like Pinchas.
b. Description of one who acts alone, detached from reality; he is like Pinchas who did not follow the crowd, but acted alone.

אַמאָל איז אַ מענטש שטאַרקער פֿון אײַזן, און אַמאָל איז ער שוואַכער פֿון אַ פֿליג.

Amol iz a mentsh shtarker fun eizen, un amol iz er shvacher fun a flig.

A person can be stronger than iron or weaker than a fly. (Strong as an ox, weak as a kitten.)

MEANING

Man can be very strong in certain circumstances, displaying surprising amounts of stamina and endurance. Sometimes, however, he shows excessive weakness, feebleness and humility.

ליגט זיך ווי אַ לעמעלע, הייבט זיך ווי אַ לייב.

Leigt zich vi a lemeleh, heibt zich vi a leib.

Lies down like a lamb and rises like a lion.

METAPHORICAL MEANING
Describes a person who appears to be sedate and restrained, but acts with daring and courage.

IN THE SOURCES
...the kid will lie down.
(Yeshayahu 11:6)

...rises like a lion.
(Bemidbar 23:24) – Before drinking wine, man is like a lamb; after imbibing it, he becomes as strong as a lion.
(Tanchuma No'ach 13)

אַ געוואָרענער איז בעסער (ערגער) ווי אַ געבאָרענער.

A gevorener iz besser (erger) vi a geborener.

One who has become that way is better (worse) than one who has been born that way.

MEANING
Positive or negative attributes and principles acquired through one's own initiative are stronger than those attained through heredity or environment.

IN THE SOURCES
"Proselytes are as hard for Israel [to endure] as a sore" – because when they act properly, the Holy One, blessed is He, punishes us for not observing the mitzvos as well as they do, even though they did not come from Jewish stock as we did.
(Tosafos Yeshanim to Yevamos 47b)

IN THE SOURCES
If a flame falls among the cedars, what would the hyssop on the wall do? If Livyasan is hauled up by a hook, what hope is there for little fish? If a hook can [catch fish] in a rushing stream, how safe can it be in marshy ponds?
(Mo'ed Katan 25b)

אַז מען שערט די שָאף,
ציטערן די לעמעלעך.

Az men shert di shof, tzittern di lemelech.

When the sheep are shorn, the lambs tremble.

METAPHORICAL MEANING
When trouble befalls the leaders, ordinary people become anxious.

IN THE SOURCES
A person's character may be identified by three things: his cup [his drinking], his pocket [charity or dealing in money matters], and his anger. (Eruvin 65b)

מ'קען נישט אַ מענטש,
ביז מ'האַנדלט נישט מיט אים.

*M'ken nisht a mentsh,
biz m'handelt nisht mit im.*

You only really know someone by having dealings with him.

MEANING
One's personality traits are better perceived in situations where one has limited control. Business dealings fall into this category.

What Is Man?

אַ מענטש איז דאָך פאָרט
נישט מער ווי אַ מענטש.

A mentsh iz doch fort nisht mer vie a mentsh.

A person is still no more than a person.
(He's only human.)

MEANING
Resignation to the fact that man has intrinsic limitations.

IN THE SOURCES
The letters of the word Adam (אדם, "man") indicate אפר, דם, מרה – *dust, blood, and gall.* (Sotah 5a)

A living man is a slave to his instincts and his Creator. (Yalkut Iyov 896)

אַ מענטש איז נישט קיין מלאך.

A mentsh iz nisht kein malach.

Man is not an angel.

MEANING
Being only flesh and blood, man has limitations and cannot be expected to act like an angel.

WORDS OF OUR SAGES
One thing I learned in Kotzk is that a man is a man and an angel is an angel. However, if man so desires, he can be more than an angel! (R' Leibeleh Eiger)

IN THE SOURCES
Do not lead us into...trial or disgrace. (Siddur)

מ'זאָל נישט געפּרובט ווערן מיט וואָס אַ מענטש קען געוויינט ווערן.

M'zoll nisht geprobt verren mit vos a mentsh ken geveint verren.

May we never have to endure all that we can learn to bear.

MEANING
Despite man's ability to adjust to even the most trying of situations, it is better not to be put to the test.

IN TALES OF THE CHASIDIM
R' Simchah Bunim of Przysucha used to tell the following parable:

There was a king who loved his only son and granted him his every wish. However, the son, an ingrate, rebelled against his father, who became angry and drove him away.

Years went by. The king's anger subsided and his heart yearned for his only son. He asked his chief minister to look for him and bring him back. After a thorough search the prince was located in the tavern of a distant village, barefoot and tattered.

The minister introduced himself as the king's messenger and asked the son how he was. "Excellent!" answered the ex-prince. "I lack nothing, but I would be very happy if I had a woolen coat and a pair of boots."

Upon hearing these words, the minister burst into tears: If the fastidious, spoiled prince could get used to such a way of life, there's no limit to the deprivation and suffering to which man can adapt, instead of trying to extricate himself.

(Based on Siach Sarfei Kodesh I, 244)

What Is Man?

דאָס אויג דערציילט וואָס דאָס האַרץ מיינט.

Dos oig dertzeilt vos dos hartz meint.

The eyes express what's in the heart.

MEANING
One's facial expression betrays one's thoughts, feelings, and desires.

IN THE SOURCES
The expression of their faces accuses them. (Yeshayahu 3:9)

בושה טוט וויי.

Busheh tut vei.

Shame hurts.

MEANING
Shame is very hurtful to the psyche. (We must therefore take care not to embarrass anyone.)

IN THE SOURCES
He who publicly shames his fellow is as though he shed blood. (Bava Metzi'a 58b)

Personal humiliation hurts more than bodily pain. (Sanhedrin 45a)

B. DIFFERENCES BETWEEN A WISE PERSON AND A FOOL

IN THE SOURCES
Even if you pound the fool in a mortar...his folly will not leave him. (Mishlei 27:22)

WORDS OF OUR SAGES
"Wisdom is superior to folly as light is superior to darkness." (Koheles 2:13) – Light: it can blind, or illuminate to a greater or lesser degree. Not so darkness: it always darkens in the same measure. A wise person may be one who sparkles intellectually, or may reveal a little and conceal twice as much. Not so the fool: he is always a fool!
(R' Levi Yitzchak of Berditchev)

קאָך דעם פּויער זיס און זויער,
וועט ער בלייבן פּויער.

*Koch dem poier zis un zoier,
vet er bleiben poier.*

Whether marinated or sugar coated, an ignoramus remains an ignoramus.
(Born a fool, always a fool.)

METAPHORICAL MEANING
External modifications cannot change one's coarse-grained nature.

IN THE SOURCES
Here is a table, meat, and knife, yet we have no mouth to eat! (Kiddushin 46a)

ווי אַ נאַר אויפֿן מאַרק

Vi a nar oifn mark

As a fool in the marketplace

METAPHORICAL MEANING
Criticism directed at one who lacks the tools to take advantage of opportunities open before him.

צו באַרשט דאַרף מען קיין ציינער האָבן.

Tzu borsht darf men kein tzeiner hobben.

One needs no teeth to drink borsht.

METAPHORICAL MEANING
One doesn't need an especially sharp eye to discern things that are perfectly clear.

IN THE SOURCES
This is known even to small school children. (Berachos 5a)

Even at a great distance [and while it is still dark] one recognizes a friend whom he sees often. (Yerushalmi Berachos 1:2)

מ'דאַרף נישט זיַין שיין, מ'דאַרף נישט זיַין קלוג, מ'דאַרף נאָר האָבן אַ גוטן מזל!

M'darf nisht zein shein, m'darf nisht zein klug, m'darf nor hobben a guten mazel!

You need be neither pretty nor clever, only lucky!

MEANING
A person's mazal (planetary influence) affects his life more than his competencies.

IN THE SOURCES
Bread is not won by the wise, nor wealth by the intelligent. (Koheles 9:11)

Everything depends on mazal. (Zohar, Naso, 134)

Mazal gives wisdom, mazal gives wealth. (Shabbos 156a)

WORDS OF OUR SAGES
It is better to have been born in a propitious hour than to good parental stock. (Rabbi Avraham ben Ezra)

WORDS OF OUR SAGES

There is a cure for every illness but the fool's.
(R' Shmuel Ha-Naggid)

אַ קראַנקער וועט געזונט ווערן,
אַ שיכּור וועט זיך אויסניכטערן,
אָבער אַ נאַר וועט בלײַבן אַ נאַר.

A kranker vet gezunt verren, a shikker vet zich oisnichtern, ober a nar vet bleiben a nar.

A sick person gets better,
a drunk sobers up,
but once a fool always a fool.

MEANING

An expression of disappointment or resignation to a situation which is similar to that of the fool; despite all the prospects for change, it seems that the fool is incorrigible.

די נאַרישקייט, אפֿילו עס געלינגט,
איז עס דאָך אַ נאַרישקייט.

*Di narishkeit, afilu es gelingt,
iz es doch a narishkeit.*

Folly, even when successful,
is still folly.

MEANING

The quality of a deed is not measured by how successful it was.

What Is Man?

וועֶן דער נאַר וואָלט נישט געווען
מײַנער, וואָלט איך אויך געלאַכט.

*Ven der nar volt nisht geven meiner,
volt ich oich gelacht.*

Had the fool not belonged to me, I would have laughed as well.

METAPHORICAL MEANING
Explains why it is hard for a person to join in when others are laughing at something ridiculous that happened to him: When a person feels the "funny" deed has hurt him, or was done by someone close to him, he is not in a laughing mood.

IN THE SOURCES
One who has been stabbed, or is otherwise in pain, cannot hear the music.
(Beginning of Eichah Rabbah 12)

אַז מ'שיקט אַ נאַר אויפן מאַרק,
פֿרייען זיך די קרעמער.

*Az m'shikt a nar oifn mark,
freien zich di kremer.*

When a fool is sent to market, the shopkeepers rejoice. (A fool and his money are soon parted.)

METAPHORICAL MEANING
The fool's weaknesses may cause him to be exploited by scoundrels.

IN THE SOURCES

Say to wisdom, "You are my sister," and call understanding, "Friend." – Always attach yourself to wisdom and understanding.
(Ralbag to Mishlei 7:4)

WORDS OF OUR SAGES

Wisdom is a twin of the Torah.
(R' Shem Tov of Falaquera)

All positive mitzvos of the Torah cry out, "Be wise." And all negative mitzvos proclaim, "Don't be a fool!"
(R' Simchah Bunim of Przysucha)

WORDS OF OUR SAGES

Ten wise men were needed to save Sodom from being destroyed, but it takes only one fool to destroy the whole world.
(R' Menachem Mendel of Kotzk)

One fool can ruin what a thousand wise men can't fix. (Ya'avetz)

וואו ס'איז תורה דארט איז חכמה.

Vu s'iz Torah dort iz chochmah.

Where Torah is, there is wisdom.

MEANING
An appreciation of the fact (surprising, to some) that one who studies Torah has much wisdom.

אַז אַ נאַר וואַרפט אַרײַן אַ שטיין אין וואַסער, קענען אים צען קלוגע נישט אַרויסנעמען.

Az a nar varft arein a shtein in vasser, kennen im tzen klugge nisht aroisnemmen.

When a fool casts a stone into a well, ten wise men will not be able to fish it out.

METAPHORICAL MEANING
The fool's destructive powers are much greater than the wise person's restorative ones.

אַ פּיקח ווייסט ווי אַרויסצוגיין פון אַ בלאָטע; אַ חכם גייט באַלד נישט אַרײַן.

A pikei'ach veist vi aroistzugein fun a blotte; a chochem geit bald nisht arein.

A clever person knows how to get out of the mud; a wise one never gets into it.
(Think before you act.)

METAPHORICAL MEANING
A clever person knows how to solve problems; better is the wise one who knows how to avert them.

IN TALES OF THE CHASIDIM
R' Yisrael of Ruzhin and R' Meir of Przemyslany met at the crossroads.

The former asked the latter: "I am traveling in a carriage drawn by four horses, whose combined strength will be able to pull it out of the mud if the need arises. You, who are traveling in a one-horse carriage, what would you do if it were to sink?"

Answered R' Meir: "Since my lone horse is not strong enough to pull me out of the mud, I am very careful not to enter into it and sink."
(Or Ha-Meir, p. 16)

IN THE SOURCES
Who is wise? He who discerns what is about to come to pass. (Tamid 32a)

Wise is he who knows what will happen at the end of what is just beginning. (Yerushalmi Sotah 5)

IN THE SOURCES
If he merits it, he toils in Torah; if not, he works the land. (Bereishis Rabbah 13:7)

אײַנער אַ קנאַק מיטן בײַטש,
דער צווייטער מיט די גמרא.

*Einer a knak mit'n beitch,
der tzveiter mit die Gemoro.*

One dispenses lashes, the other disseminates Gemara.

METAPHORICAL MEANING
Everyone operates in his area of expertise and achievement.

IN THE SOURCES
So I reflected: "The fate of the fool is also destined for me; to what advantage, then, have I been wise?" (Koheles 2:15)

וואָס טויג מיר די חכמה, אַז די נאַרישקייט געלינגט?

*Vos toig mir di chochmah,
az di narishkeit gelingt?*

Why be wise if foolishness works?
(Where ignorance is bliss, 'tis folly to be wise.)

MEANING
A protest against the fool's success.

יעדער נאַר האָט שׂכל פֿאַר זיך.

Yeder nar hot seichel far zich.

Every fool can take care of himself.

MEANING
Out of necessity, even a fool finds a way to meet his essential needs.

IN THE SOURCES
Elijah the Prophet came upon a hunter who was laying traps in the forest and asked him: "Why do you spend your days on matters that have to do with with transient life, rather than on Torah study through which one attains eternal life?"
Answered the hunter: "I am ignorant and illiterate and unable to learn and understand."
"I see that you know your job well. Since you were not born a hunter, how did you learn that skill?" asked Elijah.
"Poverty taught me," replied the hunter.
Elijah then responded: "If your soul felt distress because you are straying far away from the Creator, like the pressure you feel to satisfy your hunger, that distress would show you how to learn Torah and come closer to Hashem."
(Tanna d'vei Eliyahu)

בעסער ביַי אַ קלוגן צו פֿאַרלירן,
איידער ביַי אַ נאַר צו געווינען.

*Besser bei a klugen tzu farliren,
eider bei a nar tzu gevinnen.*

Better to lose to the wise than to gain from the fool.

METAPHORICAL MEANING
No matter how beneficial it might appear to be, one's relationship with a fool can only be detrimental. Associating with a wise person, however, is always beneficial.

בעסער אַ פּאַטש פֿון אַ חכם,
איידער אַ קוש פֿון אַ נאַר.

Besser a patsh fun a chochem, eider a kush fun a nar.

Better a slap from a wise man than a kiss from a fool.

MEANING
See IN THE SOURCES section.

IN THE SOURCES
It is better to listen to a wise man's reproof than to listen to the song of fools.
(Koheles 7:5)

"Wounds by a loved one are trustworthy, and the kisses of an enemy are extravagant." – When one injures a loved one to set him aright, his wounds are honorable, because they are helpful in setting him on the right path. Kisses of an enemy, however, are an encumbrance, since they have no benefit.
(Metzudas David to Mishlei 27:6)

What Is Man?

אַ חכם עסט כּדי ער זאָל לעבן,
אַ נאַר לעבט כּדי ער זאָל עסן.

*A chochem est k'dei er zol leben,
a nar lebt k'dei er zol essen.*

A wise man eats to live, a fool lives to eat. *(Rav Sa'adiah Gaon)*
(Eat to live, don't live to eat.)

METAPHORICAL MEANING
Criticism of people who ascribe undue importance to the pleasure of eating.
Praise of those who are involved primarily in spiritual matters, and assign less significance to food.

WORDS OF OUR SAGES
Says the wise man: "I'll eat and perhaps I'll live." Says the fool: "I'll live and perhaps I'll eat."
(Mishlei Erev, Sec. 28)

נאַר בלייבט נאַר,
מקח בלייבט מקח.

Nar bleibt nar, mekach bleibt mekach.

A fool remains a fool, a sale remains a sale.

MEANING
Even a bizarre deal made by a fool is binding.

IN THE SOURCES
An imbecile has no remedy.
(Niddah 13b)

אַ טויטן באַווײנט מען זיבן טעג,
אַ נאַר – דאָס גאַנצע לעבן.

*A toiten baveint men ziben teg,
a nar – dos gantze leben.*

A dead person is mourned seven days, a fool – his entire life.

MEANING
Since a fool is incorrigible, he inflicts continuous grief onto everyone around him.

Interpersonal Relations

INTERPERSONAL RELATIONS

אַז מ'רעדט, דעררעדט מען זיך.

Az m'redt, derredt men zich.

In order to dialogue, you must speak.
(Speak, or forever hold your peace.)

MEANING
Only by discussing the issues is there a chance for rapprochement.

יעדער איינער לעבט בײַ דעם צווייטן אין פֿרײדן.

Yeder einer lebt bei dem tzveiten in freiden.

Everyone is happy in the eyes of others.

MEANING
Our neighbor's life appears to be more glamorous than ours, because our observations are selective and limited.

IN THE SOURCES
[Said the bird:] "You observe my food, but what about my cage?!"
(Koheles Rabbah 11:13)

IN THE SOURCES

"And they saw and they took, each man his own staff." (Bemidbar 17:24) – If bundles of everyone's troubles were to be laid one next to the other, and each person were allowed to choose one, everyone would quickly retrieve his own.
(In the name of R' Simchah Bunim of Przysucha)

Elijah came [in the guise of a mortal].... Said Rabbi Akiva to his wife, "Look, there is a man who lacks even straw!" (Nedarim 50a) – Elijah came to console them by showing them that some people had even less than they did. (Ran, ibid.)

אַלע מאָל דאַכט זיך אַז ביַי יענעם לאַכט זיך, ביז מ'מאַכט אויף די טיר, זעט מען אַז ס'איז ערגער ווי ביַי מיר.

Alleh mol dacht zich az bei yenem lacht zich, biz m'macht oif die tir, zet men az s'iz erger vie bei mir.

We imagine that others are happier than we, until their door opens and reveals that the opposite is true.
(The grass looks greener on the other side.
Also: Count your blessings.)

MEANING

A brief glimpse into the life of others can show how mistaken was our belief that their situation is better than our own.

Interpersonal Relations

דעם "אוי" קען איך אויך נישט אַוועקגעבן.

Dem "oi" ken ich oich nisht avekgeben.

I can't even contribute a groan.

MEANING

This is the expression of a person so steeped in his own adversity that he cannot even groan over others' troubles. Due to his own helplessness, he has nothing to contribute to others.

ס'איז בעסער מקנא ווי מהנה.

S'iz besser mekaneh vi mehaneh.

Better to be envied than to be a beneficiary.
(It is better to give than to receive.)

MEANING

It is better to be in an enviable situation – one that attests to affluence, rather than in one that forces dependence on others.

IN THE SOURCES
Better to be envied than pitied. (Mishlei Yisrael 5156)

IN THE SOURCES
Riches do not last forever.
(Mishlei 27:24)

עס קומט נישט קיין אייביקער רעשט.

Es kumt nisht kein eibikker resht.

One need not remain eternally beholden.

MEANING
There is a limit to how beholden one must remain to a former benefactor.

IN THE SOURCES
All Jews are considered as one; if one sins, all are responsible.
(Beis Ha-Midrash 6:84)

Such is the nature of Israel: There are among them some who have neither Torah nor good deeds. What does the Holy One, blessed is He, do about it? It is impossible to destroy them. Therefore, said He: "Let them become intertwined, so that they will atone for one another."
(Vayikra Rabbah 87)

וואָס יענעם פעלט זאָל מיר צוקומען.

Vos yenem felt zol mir tzukummen.

I wish I had what he lacks.

MEANING
A Jew's wish when confronted by his fellow's deficiencies: Since we are communally responsible to complete the Creator's work, if one Jew fails to do his part, I feel it is my obligation to fulfill it.

Interpersonal Relations

ווען וואָס אים פעלט וואָלט מיר
צוגעקומען, וואָלט איך געהאַט
צו פיל.

Ven vos im felt volt mir tzugekummen, volt ich gehat tzu fil.

If I had what he lacks, I would have too much.

MEANINGS
a. An expression meant to illustrate the extent of someone else's deficiency, whether in spiritual or material matters.
b. An indirect (and inappropriate) manner of self-praise; elevating oneself by degrading one's fellow.

וואָס מ'קען נישט דערלאַנגען
זאָל מען נישט פאַרלאַנגען.

*Vos m'ken nisht derlangen,
zol men nisht farlangen.*

Do not desire what you cannot get.

MEANING
It is best not to reach too high, for it weakens, rather than strengthens, one's resolve.

WORDS OF OUR SAGES

Do not seek what you cannot obtain.
(R' Avraham Chasdai)

Much wasted effort goes into wanting what one cannot get.
(R' Shlomo ibn Gevirol)

> **IN THE SOURCES**
> Cast not a stone into the well from which you drank.
> *(Bemidbar Rabbah 22:4)*
>
> One must be grateful to him who has done him kindness.
> *(Bereshis Rabbah 79:6)*

אַז מ׳עסט דאָם פלייש זאָל מען דאָם נישט באַזידלען.

Az m'est dos fleish zol men dos nisht bazidlen.

Do not denigrate the meat you are eating.
(Bite not the hand that feeds you!)

MEANING
Do not speak disparagingly of someone or something that benefits you.

> **IN THE SOURCES**
> (Inverse of:) Where there are no leaders ["men"], try to be one. *(Avos 2:6)*

במקום שאין איש איז אַ הערינג אויך אַ פיש.

Bemokom she'ein ish (or: az s'iz nisht do kein fish) iz a herring oich a fish.

When there is no other fish, a herring will do.
(Among the blind, a one-eyed man is king.)

METAPHORICAL MEANING
In the absence of the worthy, treat the unworthy as deserving.

אַלע דעות זאָלסטו הערן, און טוען זאָלסטו ווי דו אַליין פֿאַרשטייסט.

*Alleh dei'es zolstu heren,
un tun zolstu vi du allein farshteist.*

Solicit everyone's opinion, but act according to good sense.

MEANING
To arrive at the right decisions, listen to as much advice as possible, weigh it, and then decide for yourself.

IN THE SOURCES
Plans in counsel will succeed. (Mishlei 20:18) – Plans laid with the help of advisors will endure. (Metzudas David)

The wise man accepts advice. (Mishlei 12:15)

Salvation comes with much planning. (Ibid. 11:14)

WORDS OF OUR SAGES
The best horses need bridling; the wisest men need counsel. (Me'iri)

פֿאַר די גאַנצע וועלט קען מען נישט יוצא זײַן.

Far di gantzeh velt ken men nisht yotzeh zein.

You can't satisfy everyone. (You can't please the world.)

MEANING
Don't try to appease everyone, for that is impossible.

IN THE SOURCES
It is impossible to satisfy everyone, for there was none better for the Jews than Mordechai, yet it is stated,"He was popular with most of his brethren."
(End of Pesikta Zutarta to Esther)

WORDS OF OUR SAGES
Finding favor in the eyes of everyone is an unattainable goal; to be spared from their reproach is not possible.
(R' Moshe ben Ezra)

MAMMA USED TO SAY

IN THE SOURCES

A little sleep removes the effect of wine. (Eruvin 64b)

If your fellow calls you a donkey, put a saddle on your back. (Bava Kamma 92b)

אַז מ'זאָגט "שיכּור," ליגט מען זיך שלאָפֿן.

Az m'zogt "shikker," leigt men zich shlofen.

When people say that you are drunk, go to sleep.
(If they say the truth, believe them.)

METAPHORICAL MEANING
One must take public opinion into account.

IN THE SOURCES

The favor of the wicked is evil for the righteous. (Yevamos 103a)

Better is the curse that Achiyah the Shilonite pronounced on Israel than the blessing with which the wicked Bil'am blessed them. (Ta'anis 20a)

בעסער פֿון אַ גוטן מענטש דאָס ערגסטע איידער פֿון אַ שלעכטן דאָס בעסטע.

Besser fun a guten mentsh dos ergste eider fun a shlechten dos beste.

Better the worst of a good person than the best of a bad one.

MEANING
Collaboration with good people always yields good results, while the opposite is true of associating with evil persons.

אין וועלכע שול מ'איז דאָ, אַזאַ קדושה טאַנצט מען.

In velcheh shul m'iz do, aza k'dushah tantzt men.

Follow the local synagogue's custom when saying "kedushah" there.
(When in Rome, do as the Romans do.)

METAPHORICAL MEANING
Accustom yourself to the practices of the local community, and do not separate yourself from it.

IN TALES OF THE CHASIDIM
Several years after the death of R' Zvi Hirsch of Chortkov, R' Levi Yitzchak of Berditchev spent a Sabbath in Chortkov and prayed in the house of worship where R' Zvi Hirsch used to pray. That synagogue adhered to the Ashkenazic rite, for that was what R' Zvi Hirsch had used. R' Levi Yitzchak served as cantor and prayed in the Sephardic rite, as he was wont to do. He suddenly fell into a deep sleep and dreamed that R' Zvi Hirsch stood over him, saying: "How did you dare to change the local accepted version of prayer after I toiled so much to pave a way to heaven through which prayers said in the Ashkenazic rite could ascend?!" Flustered, R' Levi Yitzchak awoke and discontinued leading the service in the Sephardic rite.

Interpersonal Relations

IN THE SOURCES
One should never break away from custom, for when Moses ascended on high he ate no bread.
(Bava Metzia 86b)

"...and they ate."
(Bereshis 18:8) – *They [the angels] appeared to eat. From here [we learn] that one should never break away from custom.* (Rashi)

IN THE SOURCES

Both the near and the far shall scorn you, O besmirched of name....
(Yechezkel 22:5)

A good name travels from one end of the earth to the other.
(Midrash Koheles Rabbah 7:1)

For the birds in the sky will carry the utterance.
(Koheles 10:20) – *This refers to the utterance of those who speak evil gossip.*
(Yalkut Koheles 989)

אַ גוטער נאָמען גייט ווײַט; אַ שלעכטער נאָמען גייט נאָך ווײַטער.

*A guter nomen geit veit;
a shlechter nomen geit noch veiter.*

A good name travels far; a bad name travels farther. (Bad news travels fast.)

MEANING
One must be careful not to spread slander, for it has wings of its own.

IN THE SOURCES

And he [Israel] called his son Joseph [to request burial in Eretz Yisrael].... And Israel bowed down upon the head of the bed.
(Bereshis 47:29-31) – *[Joseph] had it in his power to do.*
(Rashi)

WORDS OF OUR SAGES

It is impossible to not need other people. May God spare us, however, from having to rely on scoundrels.
(R' Shlomo ibn Gevirol)

בעסער זיך צו בוקן צום קאָפּ איידער צו די פֿיס.

Besser zich tzu buken tzum kop eider tzu di fis.

It is better to bow to the head than to the feet.

METAPHORICAL MEANING
When one must lower himself and grovel to obtain something, he should try to do so before someone wise and important who has the power to help.

Interpersonal Relations

וואָס קלענער דער עולם גרעסער די שׂמחה.

Vos klener der olom, gresser die simchah.

The smaller the party, the greater the merriment.

MEANING
Words of encouragement to those whose celebration is poorly attended: When the number of participants is small, the hosts are better able to enjoy each of their guests' contributions to the festivity.

וואָס גרעסער איז בעסער.

Vos gresser iz besser.

The bigger, the better. (The more, the merrier.)

MEANING
An expression of satisfaction for a big turnout at a celebration: A large number of participants adds an extra dimension of joy to the festivities.

IN THE SOURCES

"One who is an enemy of his relatives is cruel." (Mishlei 11:17) – *This refers to one who does not share joyous occasions with his relatives.*
(Vayikra Rabbah 34:3)

IN THE SOURCES

We see that when God told him [Moshe], "Go down, for your people has become corrupt" (Shemos 32:7), *he continued holding on to the tablets and did not believe that Israel had sinned.*

He said: "If I don't see, I don't believe…"
Woe to people who give testimony to what they haven't seen…

Moshe was conveying to Israel a lesson in proper behavior: Even when you have heard something from a trustworthy individual, if you haven't personally witnessed the incident, it is forbidden to accept and act on that testimony.
(Shemos Rabbah 46:1)

WORDS OF OUR SAGES

The Torah forbids us to accept lashon hara (slander).
(Chafetz Chaim, Laws of Lashon Hara, 6)

אַז מ'וועט דיר אָנרעדן אויף יענעם, זאָלסטו נישט גלייבן ביז דו וועסט זעהן מיט דיַינע אויגן.

Az m'vet dir onreden oif yenem, zolstu nisht gleiben biz du vest zehn mit deineh oigen.

When you hear evil about someone, don't believe it until you see it.

MEANING
Don't believe rumors!

IN TALES OF THE CHASIDIM

During the dispute regarding customs at the court of the Rebbe of Ruzhin, two Shinover Chasidim happened to be in Sadigora one evening during the Selichos period.

Tired from travel, they fell asleep and did not awaken until the sun had already risen. They hurried to the house of study and peeked through the window to find out how late they were.

To their astonishment, they saw dozens of gentile peasant girls dancing in a circle in the center of the study hall. The two quickly sneaked away and hurried back to Shinova to relate to their Rebbe what they had seen, so that he might "uproot the evil from Israel."

The Shinover Rebbe listened to their story and asked them not to tell it to anyone for three whole days. Meanwhile, the Rebbe sent two of his most outstanding Chasidim to investigate the matter. Upon their return, he invited the first two to hear his worthy emissaries' report: "We arrived in Sadigora while it was yet night.

The study hall was crowded with a multitude of Chasidim who were fervently and quietly reciting Selichos. When the Rebbe came up to say 'Aneinu' all eyes filled with tears and all hearts melted like water. At prayers' end the congregation left to prepare for the morning service, and then the entrance to the house of study was closed off. We peeped through the window and saw dozens of maidservants moving the benches, wiping up the mud left by the worshippers' boots, and spreading wax on the floor. To speed up the polishing, they wrapped rags around their feet and stamped and kicked the floor until it shone as befits such a regal house of study."

At that point the Rebbe stopped them and said: "Indeed, one must not believe a report before verification by trustworthy witnesses."

אַז מ'וויינט, וויינט מען אַליין;
אַז מ'לאַכט, לאַכט די גאַנצע וועלט מיט.

*Az m'veint, veint men alein;
az m'lacht, lacht di gantzeh velt mit.*

Cry, and you cry alone; laugh, and the whole world laughs with you.

MEANING
We tend to ignore the pain of others, to avoid having to come to their aid. We are always ready, however, to freely join in their happiness.

IN THE SOURCES
Some love their neighbor when he is well-off; when he is in trouble, they pretend not to know him.
(Tanchuma Vayeshev 16)

IN THE SOURCES
[I might have said:] Let us throw a stone at the fallen.
(Kiddushin 20b)

אַ געפֿאַלענעם טרעט מען נישט מיט די פֿיס.

A gefallenem tret men nisht mit di fis.

Don't step on one who is down. (Don't rub it in.)

EXPLANATION
The Yiddish "gefallenem" has two definitions: someone who has fallen, or someone who has a feeling of inferiority. The expression applies to both.

MEANING
One must refrain from trampling upon someone who has fallen and is in danger of being stepped on, as well as from treading down, humiliating, someone who feels low, who is dispirited anyway.

IN THE SOURCES
It's a necessary evil.
(Maharsha, Bava Basra 80b)

אַז מ'דאַרף דעם גנבֿ, שנײַדט מען אים פֿון דער תּליה.

Az m'darf dem ganev, shneidt men im fun der t'liah.

If the thief is needed, he will be removed even from the gallows.

METAPHORICAL MEANING
When his services are needed, and there is no other choice, even one who has been ostracized will be rehabilitated.

Interpersonal Relations

ווען איז אַ שווערער משפט? — ווען ביידע בעלי-דין זענען גערעכט.

Ven iz a shverer mishpot? —
Ven beide baalei-din zennen gerecht.

What is a difficult case? – When both litigants are right.

METAPHORICAL MEANING
It is hard to side with one disputant when his opponent has just claims, too.

ווען איז דאָס געשעפט גוט? — ווען ביידע זענען צופרידן.

Ven iz dos gesheft gut? —
Ven beide zennen tzufriden.

When is a deal successful? – When both parties are happy.

MEANING
When partners to a transaction are both satisfied with the terms, it is a sign that the partnership is successful.

IN THE SOURCES
Come and see how the way of human beings differs from that of the Holy One, blessed is He. It is the way of human beings that when someone sells his possession to his fellow, the seller is sad and the buyer is glad. But the Holy One, blessed is He, is different. He gave the Torah to Israel and rejoiced, as it is said (Mishlei 4:2): "For I have given you a good doctrine; forsake not My Torah."
(Berachos 5a)

IN THE SOURCES

"Make your foot dear by restraining it from your neighbor's house, lest he become fed up with you and loathe you." – Give value to your feet by preventing them from frequenting your friend's home.
(Metzudas David to Mishlei 25:17)

וואו מ׳האָט דיך ליב גיי ווייניג; וואו מ׳האָט דיך פיינט גיי גאָרנישט.

Vu m'hot dich lieb gei veinig;
vu m'hot dich feint gei gornisht.

Visit your friends rarely; your enemies, never.
(Don't overstay your welcome, and don't go where you're not wanted.)

MEANING

Visit your neighbor sparingly, even if he is your friend, and refrain from even stepping into your enemy's home!

IN THE SOURCES

Do not stand in the place of great men. (Mishlei 25:6)

ווי אַ מענטש צום טיש

Vi a mentsh tzum tish

As one invited to the table

METAPHORICAL MEANING

An expression that describes a person who has intruded himself into a group of people who are more important than he.

אַ גאַסט אויף אַ ווײַל און זעט אויף אַ מײַל.

A gast oif a veil un zet oif a meil.

A guest for a while can see for a mile.
(A frequent guest becomes a pest.)

MEANING
The heightened alertness of a newcomer enables him to get a quicker and better perspective about the realities in his new environment.

אַ גאַסט אויף אַ ווײל זעט אלעם דערווײַל.

A gast oif a veil zet alles derveil.

A guest for a while sees all meanwhile.

MEANING
A guest knows all about his host after even a short visit.

WORDS OF OUR SAGES

How difficult are man's ways: if he eats an unpeeled apple, he is accused of gluttony, yet if he peels it, he appears to be haughty.
(R' Noach of Lechovitz)

גייסטו פּאַמעלאַך, קריכסטו;
גייסטו שנעל, צוורייסטו די שיך.

*Geistu pamelach, krichstu;
geistu shnell, tzureistu die shich.*

Walk slowly, and you're "crawling"; walk fast, and you're "tearing your shoes." (You're damned if you do and damned if you don't.
Also: You can't win them all.)

MEANING
This is an expression of bitterness by one who thinks that whatever he does will be unsatisfactory.

אַז מ'קריגט זיך —
קושט מען זיך נישט.

Az m'krigt zich — kusht men zich nisht.

People do not kiss while quarreling.

METAPHORICAL MEANING
Don't demonstrate contradictory attitudes simultaneously.

Interpersonal Relations

אין די אויגן קען מען אַרײַנקוקן,
אָבער נישט אין האַרץ.

*In di oigen ken men areinkuken,
ober nisht in hartz.*

One can look into the eyes,
but not into the heart.
(Looks are only skin deep.)

METAPHORICAL MEANING
The eyes can reveal things about one's exterior, but it is difficult to unravel one's interior.

IN THE SOURCES
Man sees only into the eyes, but Hashem sees into the heart. (I Shmuel 16:7)

WORDS OF OUR SAGES
True, man sees only what is visible. But if his eyes could see more, they would be able to discern old people who are really young, youths who are in fact old, wealthy people who are actually poor, and poor people who are incomparably rich. They would notice that the limbs and senses of some who walk free are in actuality tightly bound, while some prisoners are as free as can be. Indeed, one can look into the eyes, but not into the heart, but what is one able to see there?!
(R' Aharon of Kozhnitz)

בעסער דער ערשטער רוגז.

Besser der ershter rogez.

Better the first anger.

MEANING
It is better to stay with a first and only grievance, than to try and cover it over with excuses that are likely to arouse more feelings of rage.

IN THE SOURCES
No leaven or honey may be turned into smoke as a fire-offering to Hashem.
(Vayikra 2:11)

"No leaven" – a person who is wholly sour; "or honey" – a person who is completely sweet. Neither of these can come close to Hashem. One must possess everything in the right measure! (Sefer Ha-Toledos)

זײַ נישט צו זיס מ'זאָל דיך נישט אויפעסן; זײַ נישט צו ביטער מ'זאָל דיך נישט אויסשפּײַען.

Zei nisht tzu zis m'zol dich nisht oifessen; Zei nisht tzu bitter m'zol dich nisht oisshpeien.

Don't be too sweet, lest you be consumed; don't be too bitter, lest you be disgorged.

MEANING
For your own good, try to maintain a balance in your relationships with others.

IN THE SOURCES
Always regard all people as robbers, but show them the same respect as to Rabban Gamliel.
(Derech Eretz Rabbah 5)

האלט מיך פאר א רב, היט מיך ווי א גנב.

Halt mich far a rov, hit mich vie a ganev.

Honor me as a rabbi – suspect me as a thief.

MEANING
Every person, as a human being, is worthy of respect. Since "man is always potentially harmful" ("mu'ad l'olam"), however, one must be wary of him.

Interpersonal Relations

לאָז נישט דעם רוגז איבערנעכטיקן ביַי דיר.

Loz nisht dem rogez ibernechtiken bei dir.

Don't go to sleep angry.

MEANING

If you don't get rid of your anger before going to bed, it will disturb your rest either by keeping you awake or by intruding upon your dreams.

METAPHORICAL MEANING

Don't let feelings of anger become entrenched; become reconciled or forgive!

IN THE SOURCES

Cease from anger and forsake wrath. (Tehillim 37:8)

Never in my life have I taken the curse of my fellow to bed with me.
(Kallah Rabbasi 3)

One must not persist in a quarrel. (Sanhedrin 110a)

וואָס פאַר אַ "גוט מאָרגן," אזאַ "גוט יאָר."

Vos far a "gut morgen," aza "gut yor."

As you wish "good morning," you will be greeted with "happy new year."
(Measure for measure. Or: Tit for tat.)

MEANING

The tone of voice with which you address others determines the tone of the response.

IN THE SOURCES

"As water reflects face to face, so the heart of man to man." – As water reflects the face you show it, so does one man's heart to another. We treat each other according to how we perceive the other's friendship toward us.
(Rashi to Mishlei 27:19)

IN THE SOURCES

Enter not into a quarrel.
(Avos d'R' Nasan 29:7)

Strife is like an opening in a dam: if is not stopped up immediately, it widens into a flood. (Sanhedrin 7a)

פֿון אַלע מחלוקות זאָלסטו זײַן רײן!
גיבסטו אַ שמעק פֿאַלסטו אַרײַן.

*Fun alleh machlokos zolstu zein rein!
Gibstu a shmek falstu arein.*

Stay clear of all disputes! Prying will entrap you.
(A soft word turns away wrath.)

MEANING

Stay away from a dispute – from its causes, its antagonists, and anything that might drag you into it!

IN TALES OF THE CHASIDIM

R' Meir of Dzhikov told the following parable to his Chasidim:

A hungry lion was looking for prey in the forest. He suddenly came upon a donkey and said to it, "How does my breath smell to you?"

The donkey grimaced and responded: "His Highness's mouth emits a terrible odor of hunger."

"You are deserving of death for having insulted the royal honor," roared the lion before devouring the donkey.

The lion continued on his way and encountered a sheep. "What does my breath smell like?" asked the lion.

"Wonderful, it has the aroma of a fine fragrance," answered the adroit sheep.

"How dare you lie so brazenly to the king of all animals?" roared the lion, and it devoured the sheep as well. Its hunger, however, was not yet satisfied. Later the lion met a fox to which it posed the same question.

The sly fox bowed and said: "Please forgive me, Your Highness, but I have had a cold for the past three days and cannot smell." Despite its hunger, the lion let the fox go!

מ'גיט זיך אַ קניפ אין באַק — אַבּי די פֿאַרב זאָל שטיין.

M'git zich a knip in bak — abi di farb zol shtein.

Pinch your cheeks – to keep them glowing.

METAPHORICAL MEANING
Avoid arousing the pity of others, even when you are down and out.

בײַ אַ געהאָנגענעם אין שטוב רעדט מען נישט אויף אַ שטריק.

Bei a gehongenem in shtub redt men nisht oif a shtrik.

Do not mention a rope in a hanged man's house.

METAPHORICAL MEANING
One must be considerate of others' sensitivities.

IN THE SOURCES

If there has been a hanging in one's family record, do not say to him, "Hang this fish up for me" (Rashi) *– The mere mention of "hanging" causes him embarrassment.*
(Bava Metzia 59b)

וואָס ס'וועט זיין מיט אלע –
וועט זיין מיט די כּלה.

*Vos s'vet zein mit alleh –
vet zein mit di kalleh.*

What will happen to everyone, will happen to this bride as well.

METAPHORICAL MEANING
The exalted should not expect special treatment forever.

אַלטע גוטע-פריינדשאַפט ראָסטעט נישט.

Alteh guteh-freindshaft rostet nisht.

Old friendships do not rust away.

METAPHORICAL MEANING
Time cannot erode true friendship.

IN THE SOURCES
Four things are better old than new: wine, fish, oil, and – more than the others – a friend. (Ta'anis 23a)

בעסער אַ ערלעכער פּאַטש, איידער אַ פֿאַלשער קוש.

Besser a erlecher patsh eider a falsher kush.

Better an honest slap than a deceitful kiss.

MEANING

People prefer an honest relationship, although less pleasant and friendly, to one that appears friendly but is full of hypocrisy and deceit.

IN THE SOURCES

"Faithful are wounds inflicted by a loved one, but the kisses of an enemy are superfluous." (Mishlei 27:6) – A loved one's corrective wounds show loyalty, because they help their recipient to improve his ways. Given by an enemy, however, even many kisses are a burden, because they are of no benefit.
(Metzudas David)

קיינער ווייסט נישט וועמען דער שוך קוועטשט.

Keiner veist nisht vemen der shuch kvetsht.

No one knows whose shoe pinches.

METAPHORICAL MEANING

Favorable outward appearances may mask inner suffering.

IN THE SOURCES

[Said the bird:] *"You observe my food, but what about my cage?!"*
(Koheles Rabbah 11:13)

IN THE SOURCES
No one can see the guilt of one whom he loves, or the merit of one whom he hates.
(Kesubos 105b)

מיט וואָס פאַר אַ פּנים מ'קוקט איינעם אָן, אַזאַ פּנים האָט ער.

Mit vos far a ponim m'kukt einem on, aza ponim hot er.

The way you look at someone, so he appears to you.

MEANINGS
a. A person's self-image is determined by society's attitudes toward him.
b. Our prejudice and feelings toward a person influence our impression of that person's behavior and speech.

IN THE SOURCES
No community is entirely rich or entirely poor.
(Yerushalmi Gittin 3:7)

קהל ווערט נישט בדלות.

Kohol vert nisht b'dalus.

A community cannot become poor.
(There's strength in numbers.)

MEANING
An acknowledgment of communal strength: A community is stronger than its individual constituents.

Interpersonal Relations

איין האַרץ פילט דאָס אַנדערע.

Ein hartz filt dos andereh.

One heart feels another.

MEANING

Your fellow feels about you as you do about him. (Feelings are mutual.)

IN THE SOURCES

And his [Jacob's] soul is bound up with his [son Benjamin's] soul.
(Bereishis 44:30)

"As water reflects face to face, so the heart of man to man." – As water reflects the face you show it, so does one man's heart to another. We treat each other according to how we perceive the other's friendship toward us.
(Rashi to Mishlei 27:19)

לעב און לאָז לעבן.

Leb un loz leben.

Live and let live.

MEANING

A request to prevent hampering the progress of others, by emphasizing everyone's right to live in peace.

גיבסטו – ביסטו.

Gibstu – bistu.

If you give, you count.

MEANING

One who bestows favors on others strengthens his standing in the community.

פֿאַר אַ הײמישען גנב קען מען זיך נישט היטן.

Far a heimishen ganev ken men zich nisht hiten.

It is difficult to protect oneself from a familiar thief.
(Save me from my relatives; I can handle my enemies.)

METAPHORICAL MEANING
It is difficult to hide things from people with whom you have a close connection.

אַז די גנבים שלאָגן זיך, קומט אַרויס די גניבה.

Az di ganovim shloggen zich, kumt arois di gneivah.

When thieves fight, the theft will be uncovered.

METAPHORICAL MEANING
Discord reveals the disputants' sins.

IN THE SOURCES
The scattering of the wicked...benefits the world.
(Sanhedrin 71b)

WORDS OF OUR SAGES
When people fight, outsiders gain.
(Chatzi Menasheh, Lech Lecha, from Yerushalmi)

Caring for the Needy

CARING FOR THE NEEDY

A. THE CHARACTER AND CONDITION OF THE POOR, THE SICK, AND THE DISTRESSED

יעדער איד האָט זיך זיַין פּעקל.

Yeder Yid hot zich zein peckel.

Every Jew has his "bundle" (burden).

METAPHORICAL MEANING
Everyone has been allocated and outfitted with a "bundle of trouble" – a quota of afflictions which he must overcome in order to achieve his purpose in life.

IN THE SOURCES
Whom Hashem favors, He tries with afflictions.
(Berachos 5a)

There is no one who has no afflictions.
(Bereishis Rabbah 93)

Afflictions come upon Israel only because of the love for Israel and for their good.
(Tanna d'vei Eliyahu Zuta 11)

WORDS OF OUR SAGES
Were we able to hang all our bundles of trouble on a nail, and then each of us select the one he prefers, I believe everyone would choose his own. Our own afflictions seem to fit us better; those of others look worse.
(R' Nasan David of Parczew)

יעדער האַרץ ליַידט זיַין שמערץ.

Yeder hartz leidet zein shmertz.

Every heart suffers its own pain.

MEANING
Every heart has its own peculiar aches, which it must personally bear in a manner that is appropriate to it.

IN THE SOURCES
The heart knows the bitterness of its soul.
(Mishlei 14:10)

WORDS OF OUR SAGES
Were I a lamp merchant, the sun would never set until I die; if I were a dealer in shrouds, people would not die as long as I lived....
(R' Avraham ben Ezra)

דָארט וואו איך בין נישטאָ, דָארט איז גוט.

Dort vu ich bin nishto, dort iz gut.

The place where I am not is a good place.
(The grass is always greener on the other side of the fence.)

MEANING
A sufferer's lament about the good that eludes him, and that is found only elsewhere.

IN THE SOURCES
"And He regarded their affliction when He heard their outcry [lit., song]." (Tehillim 106:44) – One may understand the nature of another's trouble by observing what it takes to make him rejoice and sing.
(In the name of Tzaddikim)

ווען פרייט זיך אַן אָרעמאַן? ווען ער פאַרלירט און געפינט.

Ven freit zich an oremann?
Ven er farlirt un gefint.

When does a poor man rejoice? When he finds something he has lost.

MEANING
The poor feels the joy of success only when he finds what he himself has lost.

METAPHORICAL MEANING
When does the oppressed rejoice? When his fear about an additional threatening affliction is proved wrong.

יענעמס צרות קען מען אַריבערטראָגן.

Yenem's tzores ken men aribertroggen.

It's easy to bear someone else's troubles.
(We can't feel another person's pain.)

MEANING
When troubles are someone else's, they don't feel so burdensome and painful.

געזונטע צרות קען מען אַריבערטראָגן.

Gezunteh tzores ken men aribertroggen.

"Healthy troubles" are tolerable.

METAPHORICAL MEANING
One is more accepting of hardships that are part of life's routine.

אײנער װײנט אַז די פּערל זענען שיטער, דער אַנדערער װײנט אַז דאָס לעבן איז ביטער.

*Einer veint az di perl zennen shitter;
der andereh veint az dos leben iz bitter.*

One cries over his lack of pearls; another, over life's afflictions.

MEANINGS

a. A derisive comment regarding the inequalities and gaps between haves and have-nots.

b. Criticism of those who complain about petty things: One whines excessively about his lack of something without which he can live quite comfortably, while another cries rightfully for something the lack of which prevents him from fulfilling his purpose in life.

IN TALES OF THE CHASIDIM

R' Yissachar Ber of Radoschitz used to tell the following:

When I was young I went into self-imposed exile. One evening I arrived in a distant town where there lived a Jewish baker. I asked him to put me up for the night. He agreed and made a place for me to sleep above the stove.

I arose at midnight to recite Tikkun Chatzos. I sat on the floor and began crying over the destruction of the Temple and the exile of the Divine Presence. Suddenly I heard a heart-rending sigh. Though it was totally dark, I could tell that the sighs – which were coming in ever-increasing frequency – were the baker's.

I became heartbroken and dismayed: If a village

baker, a simple man, could perform such a Tikkun Chatzos, and emit such sighs over the Temple's destruction and the exile of the Divine Presence, how could I raise my head?! And what is my self-imposed exile worth?

Then I heard the baker's wife ask him: "Why are you sighing so, Moshe?"

Between groans, he answered: "How long will you keep on cooking potatoes? It's about time you fried some cheese patties."

(Nifla'os Ha-Sabba Kaddisha 3:43)

פוילע פיש, הונדערט שמים, געלט געקאָסט, און פון שטאָט אַרויסגעוואָרפֿן.

Foileh fish, hundert shmis, gelt gekost, un fun shtot aroisgevorfen.

He ate rotten fish, was flogged a hundred times, lost money, and was thrown out of the city.

METAPHORICAL MEANING

He suffered all the negative consequences of his deed.

IN THE SOURCES

We were flogged and driven away, and they took all our money. To what can this be compared? To one who asked his servant to fetch a fish from the market. He brought him a rotten one. Said the master: "I command you to either eat the fish, receive one hundred lashes, or pay me a hundred maneh."

The servant chose to eat. He began eating, but could not finish, so he said, "I'll take the lashes."

After receiving sixty lashes, he said, "I'll pay the hundred maneh." It turned out that he ate the fish, was flogged, and paid.

(Mechilta Beshalach 14:5)

וואו מ'לייגט דעם קראַנקן איז אים נישט גוט.

Vu m'leigt dem kranken iz im nisht gut.

A sick person will feel bad wherever you lay him down.

METAPHORICAL MEANING
External modifications cannot alleviate real difficulties.

אַן אָרעמאַן איז ווי אַ לעכערדיקער זאַק.

An oremann iz vi a lecherdiker zak.

A poor man is like a bag with holes.

METAPHORICAL MEANING
A poor man is unable to hold onto his money; hence it cannot bring him good fortune.

IN THE SOURCES
"You have sowed much and brought in little; you eat without being satisfied...you clothe yourself, but no one gets warm; and he who earns anything earns it for a bag with holes." – All your earnings disappear like coins wrapped in a bundle with holes.
(Rashi to Chaggay 1:6)

שלעכט מיט דעם, ערגער אָן דעם.

Shlecht mit dem, erger on dem.

Bad with it, worse without it.

MEANING
Sometimes it is worth getting used to the bad, for it might be worse otherwise.

IN THE SOURCES
One ought to be happier with afflictions than with good, for through them he is forgiven. (Tanchuma Yisro 16)

Caring for the Needy

אַ קבצן איז אַ בעל-צדקה אויף יענעמס.

A kabtzen iz a baal-tzdokeh oif yenems.

A beggar gives charity from that of others.

MEANING
Even when the poor man gives charity, it is from others' money.

METAPHORICAL MEANING
A poor man can never show off his own.

IN THE SOURCES
Even a poor man, who himself subsists on charity, should give charity.
(Gittin 7b)

בעסער אַ סאַך דאגות, איידער איין דאגה.

Besser a sach daiges, eider ein daigeh.

Better many worries than one worry.

EXPLANATION
When a big problem arises, it commands one's full attention, such that one's other worries become insignificant in his eyes.

MEANING
Words of encouragement to one who is overwhelmed by life's many worries: Be happy that you have many worries and hope that they do not become reduced to one.

IN THE SOURCES

Some desire, but have not the means; others have the means, but not the desire.
(Chullin 7b)

אײנער האָט קיין אַפּעטיט צום עסן, דער אַנדערער האָט קיין עסן צום אַפּעטיט.

Einer hot kein appetit tzum essen; der andereh hot kein essen tzum appetit.

One has no appetite for his food; another, no food for his appetite.

METAPHORICAL MEANING
Many conditions – even paradoxical ones – can cause a sense of deficiency.

IN TALES OF THE CHASIDIM
When he was hungry, R' Zusia of Hanipoli used to say the following with joy:
"I thank You, Master of the universe, for the hunger and appetite You have given me. There are many people in the world who can afford every delicacy, but they are sick and lack an appetite. I, however, am healthy, and I thank You therefore for the feeling of hunger that fills me."

וואו האָט אַ הונט אַ הויז?!

Vu hot a hunt a hoiz?!

Where does a dog have a home?! (It's a dog's life.)

METAPHORICAL MEANING
Where can the poor man find rest?!

דעם דלות וועט מיר קיינער נישט צוגנבענען.

Dem daless vet mir keiner nisht tzuganvenen.

No one can steal my poverty.

MEANING

Unlike the rich, who live in constant fear of being robbed, the poor live a more tranquil life. Others cannot steal what they do not have.

ווען עסט אן אָרעמאַן אַ הון? אָדער ווען ער איז קראַנק, אָדער ווען די הון איז קראַנק.

Ven est an oreman a hun? Oder ven er iz krank, oder ven di hun iz krank.

When does a poor man eat chicken? When either he is sick or the chicken is sick.

EXPLANATION

When ill, a poor man will have a chicken slaughtered to help him get well, despite his privation. When the chicken is sick, he has to hurry and slaughter it before it becomes "treif."

METAPHORICAL MEANING

Even the tiniest bit of pleasure in a poor man's life is due to misfortune.

IN THE SOURCES

Make us not be in need...of the gifts of human hands, or of their loans.
(Birkas Hamazon)

"[Hashem] will judge every hidden deed." (Koheles 12:14) – This refers to one who gives alms to a poor person in public. Rabbi Yannai once saw someone give a zuz to a poor person publicly, and said to him: "It would have been better had you not given him, than to have given him publicly and embarrassed him." (Chagigah 5a)

מ'שטאַרבט נישט פאַר הונגער,
מ'שטאַרבט פאַר בושה.

M'shtarbt nisht far hunger,
m'shtarbt far boosheh.

One does not die of hunger; one dies of shame.

MEANING
Hunger did not kill the poor man. Being ashamed to collect for his livelihood did it.

IN TALES OF OUR SAGES
During the funeral of one of Kovno's poor – a previously rich Jew who had become destitute – the mourners were bewailing the fact that he had once been able to enjoy all life's pleasures, yet he had died of hunger.

R' Yisrael of Salant responded: "He did not die of hunger, but rather because of shame. Had he overcome his vanity and accepted charity as a necessary evil, he would not have come to such hunger."

IN THE SOURCES

There are three whose life is no life: He who is dependent on his neighbor's table.... (Beitzah 32b)

When a man eats of his own labor, his mind is at ease; of others', his mind is not at ease. (Avos d'Rabbi Nasan 31)

פֿרעמד ברויט רייסט אין האַלז.

Fremd broit reist in halz.

Someone else's bread burns the throat.

MEANING
He who subsists by means of others' gifts is never completely satisfied.

אַז דאָס אומגליק דאַרף איינעם
טרעפֿן, טרעפֿט עס אים אויפֿן
גלײַכן וועג.

*Az dos umglik darf einem treffen,
treft es im oifen gleichen veg.*

When tragedy has to strike,
it will strike even on a straight road.

(It's "bashert" [destined to be].)

METAPHORICAL MEANING
Even taking a safe route will not protect one from a misfortune decreed by Heaven.

IN THE SOURCES
*Said Rabbi Yochanan: "A man's feet are responsible for him: they lead him to where he is wanted" (by the Angel of Death, when he must return his soul).
King Solomon had two scribes who attended him. One day Solomon saw that the Angel of Death was sad. He asked him, "Why are you sad?"
"Because Heaven is demanding from me the two who are sitting before you," answered the Angel of Death.
Solomon then gave them over to the demons to take them to the district of Luz, where death did not reign. However, when they reached the gates of Luz they died.
The next day Solomon saw that the Angel of Death was happy. "Why are you happy?" asked Solomon. Answered the angel: "You [helped me, for you] sent them to where I was commanded to take their lives." (Based on Sukkah 53a)*

B. SUPPORT AND GUIDANCE TO THOSE WHO PERFORM KINDNESSES

IN THE SOURCES

If you have nothing to offer him, comfort him with words. (Vayikra Rabbah 34)

He who shows his teeth [i.e., smiles] to his friend is better than one who gives him milk to drink. (Kesubos 111b)

He who gives a perutah to a poor man receives six blessings, but he who offers him words of comfort receives eleven blessings. (Bava Basra 9b)

WORDS OF OUR SAGES

Sometimes there is reason to envy the rich: They contribute reluctantly and are dragged into Paradise against their will. (R' Shlomo of Radomsk)

אַז מ'קען נישט העלפן מיט געלט דאַרף מען כאָטש העלפן מיט אַ קרעכץ.

Az m'ken nisht helfen mit gelt, darf men chotsh helfen mit a krechtz.

If you can't help with money, at least help with a sigh.

MEANING
Sharing someone's burden may be accomplished even through sympathy alone.

אַ גביר שלעפט מען מיט געוואַלד אין גן-עדן אַרײַן.

A gvir shlept men mit gevald in Gan-Eden arein.

A rich man is dragged into Paradise against his will.

MEANING
This is a statement criticizing the rich who give charity reluctantly. (Getting charity from him is like pulling teeth.)

"ונתנו" מאַכט צוריק אויך "ונתנו".
"Venasnu" macht tzurik oich "venasnu."

"Venasnu" backwards is also "venasnu" (in Hebrew).
(To give is to receive twofold.)

IN THE SOURCES
Each shall give a ransom for himself. (Shemos 30:12)

EXPLANATION
The letters ונתנו (meaning, "shall give") spell the same word forwards and backwards.

MEANING (IN THE WORDS OF THE COMMENTATORS)
It reads ונתנו backwards as well. This teaches us that whatever one gives to charity will come back to him; he will lack nothing because of it.
(Ba'al Ha-Turim to Shemos 30:12)

It reads the same way backwards, because "he who is merciful to others, mercy is shown to him by Heaven." *(Shabbos 151b)* – In the same way and measure that one is merciful to others, Heaven will have mercy on him.
(In the name of R' Menachem Mendel of Rimanov)

He who is merciful to others – others will have mercy on him in his hour of need. It is as Rabbi Chiya said to his wife: When a poor man comes, hurry to offer him bread, so that others may be quick to offer it to your children.
(Based on Shabbos 151b)

MAMMA USED TO SAY

WORDS OF OUR SAGES
The dynamics of giving and taking are at the root of every attribute and action. One must be aware that there is no middle road concerning this, because one's soul always aspires toward one or the other...With every deed, word or thought one is either kindly giving or selfishly taking.
(Michtav Me-Eliyahu 1:Chessed)

IN THE SOURCES
If you wish to be loved by your fellow, involve yourself in helping him.
(Derech Eretz Zuta 2)

א נעמער איז נישט קיין געבער.

A nemmer iz nisht kein gebber.

A taker is not a giver.

EXPLANATION
The Yiddish word "gebber" means giver. However, it also sounds like "gibber," (גבור, which means "strong"). The expression, therefore, has two meanings:
a. One who tends to always take to himself is not disposed to giving to others.
b. One who takes is not strong (a gibber), but weak.

צדקה צו געבען און ליב צו האָבן קען מען נישט נייטן.

Tzdokeh tzu geben un lib tzu hoben ken men nisht neiten.

Charity and love cannot be imposed by force.

MEANING
One cannot be coerced to express feelings of compassion or love; these must be aroused through education and character development.

Caring for the Needy

אויף אַן אָרעמאַן קען מען זיך לײַכט פֿאַרזינדיקן.

Oif an oremann ken men zich leicht farzindiken.

It is easy to sin in dealing with a poor person.

MEANING
One must be careful neither to hurt a poor person, nor to delay in providing his needs.

IN THE SOURCES
For he is needy...else he will cry to Hashem against you, causing you to have a sin.
(Devarim 24:15)

Said his disciples [to Nachum Ish Gamzu, who was suffering terribly]: "Master, why has this happened to you?" He responded: "I brought it all upon myself. I was once traveling with three laden donkeys...when a poor man stopped me on the road and said, 'Master, please give me something to eat.' I replied to him, 'Wait until I unload the donkey.' He died before I unloaded the donkey. I prostrated myself on him and cried out, 'May my eyes that had no pity on yours become blind....'"
(Ta'anis 21a)

דאָרט װוּ עס איז אָנגעװײטיקט דאָרטן טשעפּעט זיך.

Dort vu es iz ongeveitikt dorten tsheppet zich.

They always touch where it hurts.

MEANING
Sore spots are very vulnerable to pain.

אַ קראַנקן פֿרעגט מען,
אַ געזונטן גיט מען.

A kranken fregt men, a gezunten git men.

One must ask a sick person, but give to a healthy one.

MEANING

Before assisting someone who is ill, find out from him whether you are likely to cause him harm due to his infirmities. Help a healthy person, however, without asking, lest he refuse out of politeness.

אַ געשלאָגענעם װײַזט מען
קיין שטעקן נישט.

A geshloggenem veizt men kein shtekken nisht.

Don't show a rod to someone who has been beaten.

(Don't kick a man when he's down.)

METAPHORICAL MEANING

One must not pick on another person's sensitivities, even by allusion.

זאָלסט בעסער גלייבן,
און נישט צו גלייבן צוקומען.

*Zolst besser gleiben,
un nisht tzu gleiben tzukummen.*

Better to believe than to have to experience before believing.

MEANING

It is better to believe one who complains that he is suffering, and to help him and share in his pain, than to believe him only after having experienced similar suffering yourself.

קיינער זאָגט נישט קיין "איי"
אויב ס'טהוט אים נישט וויי.

*Keiner zogt nisht kein "ei"
oib s'tut im nisht vei.*

One does not groan unless he is in pain.

MEANING

Believe and be considerate of the suffering of one who groans.

From Planning to Doing

FROM PLANNING TO DOING

A. PLANNING AND PERFORMANCE, WILL AND ABILITY, CONFRONTING AND OVERCOMING

דער וועלער איז בעסער פון דעם קענער.

Der veller iz besser fun dem kenner.

Better the willing than the able.

IN THE SOURCES
Nothing stands in the way of will. (Based on Zohar 2:162)

MEANING
The power of the will is great, for it instills ability into the willing.

IN TALES OF THE CHASIDIM
The "Holy Yid" was walking with his disciple, R' Simcha Bunim of Przysucha. They came upon a farmer who called on them to help him, as his wagonload of hay had overturned. They told him it was beyond their power to help him. Shouted the gentile, "You don't want to, that is why you can't!" Said the "Holy Yid" to his disciple, "Do you hear what he is saying? Whoever wants to, can!"

* * *

R' Naftali Tzvi Geffen told the folowing: When I was a child, my father took me to the Sadigorer Rebbe. My father asked the Rebbe to bless me that I should *know* how to learn Torah, but the Rebbe gave me a blessing that I should *want* to learn Torah. Years passed and I came to realize that the Rebbe's blessing comprised my father's blessing and even added much more to it!

WORDS OF OUR SAGES

If one does not awaken himself, how will he be helped by remonstrance?
(Rabbeinu Yonah, Shaarei Teshuvah 2:26)

What effect does a bell have on a deaf ear?
(R' Shlomo ben Gevirol)

How will opening the eyes help a blind heart?
(R' Berechyah Ha-Nakdan)

IN THE SOURCES

Do you think I am offering you authority? I am offering you servitude!
(Horayos 10a)

וואָס נוצט ליכט און אַ בריל,
ווען דער מענטש נישט זען וויל?

*Vos nutzt licht un a bril,
ven der mentsh nisht zehn vil?*

Of what use are light and spectacles if one refuses to use his eyes?

METAPHORICAL MEANING
It is difficult to help one solve his problem without his cooperation.

"אונטערנעמען" הייסט:
זיך פֿאַרקויפֿן.

"Unternemen" heist: zich farkoifen.

Pledging yourself is selling yourself.

MEANING
One who has taken on a job must dedicate all his energy to its accomplishment.

From Planning to Doing

אַז מ'קען נישט פּולווער שמעקן — דאַרף מען אין אַ מלחמה נישט גיין.

*Az m'ken nisht pulver shmeken,
darf men in a milchomeh nisht gein.*

If you can't take the smell of gunpowder, stay out of the army.

(If you can't take the heat, stay out of the kitchen.)

METAPHORICAL MEANING
One who cannot cope with the problems that go along with the performance of a task should not take it upon himself at the outset.

אַז מ'קען נישט און מ'ווייסט נישט, נעמט מען זיך נישט אונטער.

Az m'ken nisht un m'veist nisht, nemt men zich nisht unter.

If you lack the ability and expertise, decline the job!

MEANING
Take on only those tasks for which you are qualified.

IN THE SOURCES
When you go out to battle...the officials shall further address the troops..."Is there anyone afraid and disheartened? Let him go back to his home...." (Devarim 20:1-8)

If you are strong, go and smite the bear that is attacking you.
(Bereshis Rabbah 87:3)

WORDS OF OUR SAGES
Do not try to be a judge if you are unable to punish the wicked. (Tzemach Tzedek)

A rabbi who cannot swallow needles should have nothing to do with the rabbinate.
(R' Aryeh Leib of Stanislav)

WORDS OF OUR SAGES

To follow the correct course, consult your brother or a friend. (R' Yosef Zebara)

Always seek advice and you won't go wrong.
(Ben Ha-Melech Ve-Ha-Nazir, Ch. 13)

It is like being in a maze... One walking in its paths can't tell whether he is on the right one or not, unless he recognizes those which lead to the final destination. People who control their evil inclination, however, who have already arrived there, are able to advise others...
(Messilas Yesharim, Ch. 4)

בעסער פרעגן איידער בלאנדזשען.

Besser fregen eider blonjen.

Better to ask than to err.

MEANING
It is better to solicit advice from others, despite the hardship or discomfort involved, than to err out of ignorance.

IN TALES OF THE CHASIDIM
R' Chaim of Tzanz used to tell the following parable:
A man lost his way in the thick of the forest. He wandered around for three days but could not find his way out. On the fourth day he met a traveler whom he asked excitedly, "Can you help me get out of this forest?" The latter answered, "I don't know how to get out, for I am also lost. But you were right to ask me, because I'll tell you where I have been walking, so you don't take the same route."

WORDS OF OUR SAGES

Ask someone who found out the hard way. It will save you much expense and aggravation.
(R' Avraham Chasdai)

פרעגן קאסט קיין געלט נישט.

Fregen kost kein gelt nisht.

It doesn't cost anything to ask.

MEANING
You can't lose much by investigating and asking.

פֿאַר פֿרעגן קומט קיין פּאַטש נישט.

Far fregen kumt kein patsh nisht.

It can't hurt to ask.

MEANING
No harm will befall you from asking, investigating, and seeking advice. Therefore, don't hesitate to do so.

IN THE SOURCES
A rabbi must not get angry with students who did not understand the lesson. He should rather repeat the material again and again until they fully comprehend the depths of the Halachah. Similarly, a student must not say that he has understood, when he has not, but should ask the teacher to explain the subject even several times. If the teacher becomes angry, the student should say: "Rebbe, this is Torah and I must learn it, although my mind is slow."
(Rambam, Talmud Torah 4:4)

גיי פּאַוואָליע; וועסטו גיכער אָנקומען.

Gei pavolyeh; vestu gicher onkummen.

Slow down; you'll get there faster.

MEANING
A saying in praise of patience.

WORDS OF OUR SAGES
It is harder to avoid obstacles when driving fast. The more patient one is, the better chance he has of reaching his destination.
(Mivchar Ha-Peninim, Rashbag, "Patience")

IN THE SOURCES
Pressing for results is counterproductive; success comes to him who adjusts.
(Bereshis Rabbah 64)

WORDS OF OUR SAGES
My disciples don't want what they don't have, because I teach them to want what they have.
(R' Yekusiel Yehudah of Klausenburg)

If your life is not as you will it, adjust your will to your life!
(R' Mordechai of Lechovitz)

אַז עס מאַכט זיך נישט ווי מ'וויל מוז מען וועלן ווי עס מאַכט זיך.

Az es macht zich nisht vi m'vill muz men vellen vi es macht zich.

If you don't have what you like, like what you have.

MEANING
We have to accept reality.

IN THE SOURCES
All beginnings are difficult.
(Mechilta, and Rashi to Yisro 19:5)

שווער איז נאָר דעם ערשטן מאָל.

Shver iz nor dem ershten mol.

Only the first time is hard.
(The first step is the hardest.)

MEANING
Words of encouragement for someone who is undertaking a difficult endeavor: The beginning will be hard, but things will get easier.

לאַנג געטראַכט און גוט געמאַכט.

Lang getracht un gut gemacht.

Long planned and done well.

MEANING
Words of praise for adequate planning, for it leads to better performance.

עס וועט טויגן ווי באַנקעס צו אַ טויטן.

Es vet toigen vi bankes tzu a toiten.

It will help like cupping-glasses to a dead person.
(It won't help.)

METAPHORICAL MEANING
An expression meant to prevent trying to save something lost, by using methods that are only effective when there is yet hope.

From Planning to Doing

IN THE SOURCES
Careful planning before taking action is most worthwhile and beneficial.
(Vayikra Rabbah 9:3)

Last in deed, but first in thought.
("Lecha Dodi" by R' Shlomo Alkabetz)

WORDS OF OUR SAGES
The temperate one proceeds in a level-headed way; hence he does not rush things. One who is lazy does not compose himself; therefore his behavior is hasty.
(R' Menachem Mendel of Kotzk)

MAMMA USED TO SAY

אַ גאַנצע נאַכט אויסגעבעט,
און איין שעה גוט געשלאָפֿן.

A gantzeh nacht oisgebet, un ein sho'oh gut geshloffen.

Prepared his bed all night, and slept in it one hour.

METAPHORICAL MEANING
A description of one who spent much time preparing for an action which he then performed well in a very short time.

IN TALES OF THE CHASIDIM
R' Leibel Eiger came to see his Rebbe, R' Menachem Mendel of Kotzk, before setting out to visit his grandfather, Rabbi Akiva Eiger. He asked his Rebbe what he should answer if his esteemed grandfather were to ask him why Chasidim pray late and are not careful about meeting the set times for prayer.

R' Menachem Mendel answered: It is well-known that he who sharpens his ax all day, and does his work in one hour, is paid as if he had worked all day!

IN THE SOURCES
Necessity should be neither criticized nor praised.
(In the name of the Maharsha)

אַז מ'האַקט האָלץ פֿאַלן שפּענער.

Az m'hakt holtz fallen shpenner.

Chopping wood yields splinters.

METAPHORICAL MEANING
Necessary actions sometimes cause damage or pain.

From Planning to Doing

עם העלפט נישט כאַטש שרײַ: "חי וקיים..."

Es helft nisht chotsh shrei: "Chai veKayom..."

Even screaming "Chai veKayom" won't help.

IN THE SOURCES
The Eternal One, awesome, exalted, and holy.
(Morning Service for Rosh Hashanah and Yom Kippur)

EXPLANATION
The words Chai veKayom (the Eternal One) are said in a very loud voice in the synagogue on Rosh Hashanah and Yom Kippur.

METAPHORICAL MEANING
It won't help even if you scream as loudly as one does when saying Chai veKayom.

געכאַפט דעם פיש פֿאַר דעם נעץ.

Gechapt dem fish far dem netz.

He grabbed the fish before it got caught in the net.

(Don't put the cart before the horse!)

METAPHORICAL MEANING
A description of someone who did things in the wrong order ("jumped the gun").

MAMMA USED TO SAY

איך קען זיך מײַן שטעטל
אַליין באַשטיין.

Ich ken zich mein shtetl alein bashtein.

I can protect my town myself.

METAPHORICAL MEANING
I can take care of my own affairs without assistance.

אַז מ'עסט נישט קיין קנאָבל —
שפּירט זיך נישט פֿון מויל.

*Az m'est nisht kein knobbel —
shpirt zich nisht fun moil.*

If you don't eat garlic,
your mouth won't smell bad.

METAPHORICAL MEANING
Negative results come from negative causes.

IN THE SOURCES
Rebbi came to teach his students and detected the smell of garlic. He asked that whoever had eaten garlic leave. Rabbi Chiya stood up and left, followed by everyone else. The next morning Rebbi's son Rabbi Shimon met Rabbi Chiya and said to him: "You are he who caused my father anguish [by eating garlic]?" Rabbi Chiya responded: "I would never do that!" [Lit., That would never happen.] (He did not eat it, but walked out so that everyone else would follow, to avoid the disclosure and embarrassment of the one who did.) (Sanhedrin 11a)

דער טשאָלנט איז געראָטן נאָך די געסט.

Der tsholent iz geroten noch di gest.

The cholent's success depends on the guests.

MEANING

The taste of the cholent is directly proportional to the quality of one's guests.

METAPHORICAL MEANING

This could serve as: a) a compliment to those involved in a successful endeavor, or b) a disapproval of the way something turned out because of persons involved.

אָדער עס העלפט נישט, אָדער מ'דאַרף נישט.

Oder es helft nisht, oder m'darf nisht.

Either it doesn't help, or it isn't needed.

MEANING

Expression of a wish to forego an offer of questionable help: It is not worth the effort, because it can't change anything anyway.

IN THE SOURCES
To what could Israel have been compared when they left Egypt? – To a dove that escaped from a hawk and flew into the crevice of a rock, only to find it occupied by a snake. Now caught between the hawk and the snake, what could she do? She cried out and flapped her wings, so that the owner of the dovecote would hear and come to her rescue.
(Shir Ha-shirim Rabbah 2:30)

WORDS OF OUR SAGES
The eyes are to the front, not the back. (Rambam)

נישט אַרויס און נישא אַריַין – קען קיין ערגערס נישט זיַין.

Nisht arois un nisht arein – ken kein ergers nisht zein.

Neither in nor out; it can't be worse.

METAPHORICAL MEANING
When one's path is blocked, so that he can go neither forward nor backward, or when one cannot decide which way to proceed, he is at the peak of distress.

אַ מענטש גייט נישט אַהין מיטן קאָפּ אויף צוריק.

A mentsh geit nisht ahin mitn kop oif tzurik.

One doesn't march forward facing backward. (Don't look backward!)

INSTRUCTION
Don't make yesterday's mistakes; look ahead to tomorrow!

From Planning to Doing

אַז מ'האָט נישט אין קאָפּ —
האָט מען אין די פֿיס.

Az m'hot nisht in kop — hot men in di fis.

If it's not in one's head, it will be in his feet.

MEANING

If you don't remember what you were supposed to do, you'll have to retrace your steps.

אַרײַן איז אַלע מאָל
גרינגער ווי אַרויס.

Arein iz alleh mol gringer vi arois.

Getting in is always easier than getting out.

MEANING

A comment about someone who embarked upon something under favorable terms, but later found himself in dire straits...

Alternatively: A warning against hastily accepting a task or mission: Extricating oneself from it is liable to be complicated!

IN THE SOURCES

A fox once entered a vineyard through a hole in the fence and spent three days there eating grapes. When it tried to leave, it found that the hole was too tight for its increased size. It then had to fast three days in order to get back out...
(Based on Koheles Rabbah 5)

אַראָפּ איז שווערער ווי אַראָף.

Arop iz shverer vi arof.

Coming down is harder than going up.

MEANING

It is simpler adjusting to easy and comfortable conditions than to difficult ones: It is easier getting used to riches and honor than to losing them.

ווי אַזוי קומט די קאַץ איבערן וואַסער?!

Vi azoy kumt di katz ibern vasser?!

How will the cat cross the river?!

METAPHORICAL MEANING

How does one overcome difficult obstacles?

טאָן דאַרף מען, אויפטאָן קען מען.

Tun darf men, oiftun ken men.

To act is necessary; to accomplish is possible.

MEANING

There's merit in trying even without assured results.

IN THE SOURCES

You need not complete the task, but you are not free to disregard it. (Avos 2:16)

געזאָגט — און געטאָן!

Gezogt – un geton!

Say – and do!
(No sooner said than done!)

MEANING
Actions should closely follow words.

IN THE SOURCES
Blessed is He Who says and performs. (Metaphorically: Blessed is he who promptly fulfills his word.)
(From the blessing "Baruch She-amar")

ס'רעדט זיך לײַכטער ווי ס'מאַכט זיך.

S'redt zich leichter vi s'macht zich.

It's easier said than done.

MEANING
A statement meant to restrain someone who expects things to get done without considering the difficulties involved.

וואָס מ'כאַפט נישט אַרײַן האָט מען נישט.

Vos m'chapt nisht arein hot men nisht.

Opportunity only knocks once.

INSTRUCTION
Take advantage of opportunities.

IN THE SOURCES
Hashem your God will bless you in all that you do. (Devarim 15:18)

Man must toil and do with both hands, and the Holy One, blessed is He, will send His blessing. (Tanchuma Vayetze 13)

מ'מוז טאָן, און דער אויבערשטער זאָל אויפטאָן.

M'muz tun, un der Oibershter zol oiftun.

Let us do our part, and God will do His.

MEANING
Man must make an effort, and God will bless his actions accordingly.

IN THE SOURCES
Man's feet are his guarantors. (Sukkah 53a)

דאָרט וואו דער קאָפּ דאַרף ליגן דאָרט שלעפּן די פֿיס.

Dort vu der kop darf ligen dort shleppen di fis.

Man's feet pull him to where his head must lie.

METAPHORICAL MEANING
Man's deeds lead him to where it has been decreed that he should die.

From Planning to Doing

אַז מ'לייגט נישט אַריין,
נעמט מען נישט אַרױס.

Az m'leigt nisht arein, nemt men nisht arois.

If you put nothing in, you can take nothing out.
(As you sow, so shall you reap.)

METAPHORICAL MEANING
Achievement requires effort.

IN THE SOURCES
If someone were to tell you, "I toiled but did not find," don't believe him; "I did not toil but found," don't believe him; "I toiled and found," believe him!
(Megillah 6b)

The reward is in direct proportion to the effort.
(Avos 5:26)

געבענטשט זענען די הענט
װאָס טוען זיך אַלײן.

Gebensht zennen di hent vos tuen zich allein.

Blessed are the hands that accomplish their own needs.

MEANING
A statement of admiration and blessing directed to one who works to meet his own needs: Whatever one does for himself, he does with devotion and dedication, and it will be blessed.

IN THE SOURCES
...and to bless all the work of your hand.
(Devarim 28:12)

If I am not for me, who will be for me?! (Avos 1:14)

When you eat the labor of your hands, you will be happy. (Tehillim 128:2)

Blessing rests only upon man's handiwork.
(Tosefta Berachos 6)

נישט אַזוי שנעל טוט זיך ווי עס רעדט זיך.

Nisht azoy shnell tut zich vi es redt zich.

Things are not as quickly done as they are spoken.

MEANING
A statement intending to slow down someone who has not carefully estimated the time it should take to accomplish the task at hand.

אָפּגעטאָן איז אָפּגעטאָן.

Opgeton iz opgeton.

What's done is already done.

MEANING
One can't undo what has already been done, even though it seems that it would have been better left undone.

IN THE SOURCES
What's done cannot be undone.
(Based on Rosh Hashanah 29b)

קריכן אויף גלייכע ווענט

Krichen oif gleicheh vent

To climb up straight walls

METAPHORICAL MEANING
A description of doing something impossible.

א ברייטע טיר אריין,
א שמאלע טיר ארוים.

A breiteh tir arein, a shmoleh tir arois.

Into a wide door,
and out of a narrow one.

(Wide horizons,
small accomplishments.)

MEANING
A description of one who came into a situation, or began an action, under comfortable conditions, only to leave or finish it under stress.

ווי קומט אַ בוידעם צום קלאָץ?!

Vi kumt a boidem tzum klotz?!

How will the attic reach the beam?!

METAPHORICAL MEANING
A statement of wonderment: How can one bring the objective nearer?!

מ'קען דעם קעצל'ס ווײדל נישט צובינדן.

M'ken dem ketzel's veidel nisht tzubinden.

You can't tie the cat's tail.
(Don't attempt the impossible.)

METAPHORICAL MEANING
It's impossible to carry it out.

IN THE SOURCES
Can a man stoke up a fire in his bosom, and his clothes not be burned? (Mishlei 6:27)

מיט פרעמדע הענט איז גוט פייער צו שייערן.

Mit fremdeh hent iz gut feier tzu sheiern.

Stoke up a fire with someone else's hands.

INSTRUCTION
Use someone else to do only that which may harm you (were you to do it yourself). Do everything else yourself, for then it will be blessed.

B. WORK AND THE PROFESSIONS

נישט געקענט שרייבן,
נישט געקענט לעזן,
און פארט אַ מייסטער געוועזן.

*Nisht gekennt shreiben, nisht gekennt lezen,
un fort a meister gevezen.*

He couldn't read or write,
yet he became a senior official.

METAPHORICAL MEANING
A description of one who attained a respectable position, despite having few qualifications.

מער שוחטים ווי הינער

Mer shochtim vi hiner

More slaughterers than chickens
(More chiefs than Indians)

METAPHORICAL MEANING
Criticism of the fact that there is a plethora of degree-holders and officials, compared to the number of those whom they serve.

מיט אַ גרויסן דאָקטער גייט אַ גרויסער מלאך.

Mit a groissen dokter geit a groisser malach.

A big doctor is accompanied by a big angel.

MEANING

The secret to a great doctor's success is the great angel, sent by God, to help him. (We must, therefore, seek the opinion of a great doctor.)

IN TALES OF THE CHASIDIM

A Jew presented a note to R' Dov Ber of Mezritch. The Maggid looked at the name inscribed therein, raised his eyes and said: "Know, my son, that it is not the doctor who heals, but the angel that accompanies him. The more successful the doctor, the greater is his accompanying angel!"

The Jew was shocked by those words, because his note mentioned no illness or pain... Shortly after returning home, he took ill, and his illness became so severe that his doctors gave up hope. His worried relatives then heard about the approach of the king's entourage, accompanied by the king's physician, renowned for his medical proficiency. They rushed out to see the doctor, begged him to see the patient, and offered him a substantial fee.

Upon observing the patient's critical condition, the doctor became angry that they troubled him to come and see such a critically ill person who had hardly any remaining vital signs. Nevertheless, he urged them to hurry and get some special medicines that might help the patient.

From Planning to Doing

While they were still trying to obtain the medications, the patient's condition suddenly began to improve, his temperature fell, and he began to regain consciousness. By the time the medicines arrived, they were hardly needed!

A short time later, the patient was able to sit up in bed and tell the physician what the Maggid of Mezritch had told him about the great angel that accompanies great doctors... All those present in the room "felt" the angel's presence. The physician, too, was impressed by what had been said, for who could testify to its veracity better than he? (Those words even aroused him to return to his Jewish heritage.)

גוט איז די דאָקטוירים; זייערע
מעלות פֿאַרקלינגען די וועלט,
זייערע פֿעלערן פֿאַרדעקט די ערד.

Gut iz di doktorim; zeiere maalos farklingen di velt, zeiere feleren fardekt di erd.

How lucky are doctors: everyone hears about their successes, but their failures are buried.

MEANING
It's convenient when one can publicize his successes and cover up his failures.

דאָקטוירים ווייסן אַ קרענק.

Doktorim veissen a krenk.

Doctors know all about illness.
(Doctors know nothing.)

EXPLANATION
"Krenk" has two meanings in Yiddish: illness or, sarcastically, nothing. Each applies to a different sort of doctor.

צו ווערן אַ רביצין איז לייכטער ווי צו ווערן אַ רב.

Tzu verren a rebbetzin iz leichter vi tzu verren a rov.

It's easier to become a rebbetzin than a rabbi.

MEANING
One must study and work hard to become a rabbi. To become a rebbetzin, one need only marry a rabbi.

METAPHORICAL MEANING
Some attain a degree (or a title) by hard work. Others attain it easily, through "connections," family, or social position.

מיט וואָס איינער האַנדלט שלעפּט זיך אים נאָך.

Mit vos einer handelt shlept zich im noch.

One's occupation follows him around.

MEANING
One's occupation affects one's thoughts and deeds.

IN TALES OF THE CHASIDIM
A Chasid came to his Rebbe and excitedly told him at length all about the handsome, strong horse and wagon he had acquired, and the great hope he was putting on them to improve his livelihood.

The Rebbe cast a sorrowful look upon the young scholar, who had previously devoted his days and nights to Torah study, and now appeared to be totally immersed in his horse, and said: "What a pity! You have turned your head – that was like a house full of books – into a barn; now the horse occupies it fully..."

(Siach Sarfei Kodesh 5:24)

IN THE SOURCES
Every artisan talks about his trade.
(Zohar Mishpatim 107a)

Every Word Counts

EVERY WORD COUNTS

A. SPEECH AND SILENCE

די אויערן מוזן הערן וואָס דאָס מויל רעדט.

Di oiern muzen heren vos dos moil redt.

The ears must hear what the mouth utters.

(Do you hear what you're saying?)

INSTRUCTION
Be careful of what you say.

> **IN THE SOURCES**
> *Let your ears hear what your mouth emits.*
> (Berachos 13a)

אַ װאָרט אויפֿן אָרט

A vort oifen ort

A word in its place

MEANING
A word has special value when it is said at the right place and time, in the proper context, to the right audience, etc.

> **IN THE SOURCES**
> *A man rejoices in what he says; how good is something at the proper time.* (Mishlei 15:23)
>
> *When does a man rejoice in what he says? When it is said at the proper time!* (Eruvin 54a)

WORDS OF OUR SAGES

Your secret is your prisoner; if you reveal it, you will become its prisoner.
(Mivchar Ha-Peninim 29:6)

After saying something, it has control over me; before saying it, I have control over it. (Sefer Chasidim 86)

דאָס וואָרט — אינעם מויל איז אַ האַר, פונעם מויל איז אַ נאַר.

Dos vort — innem moil iz a har, funnem moil iz a nar.

While the word is in your mouth, you are in command; letting it escape may render you a fool.

MEANING

Before expressing your thought, you are in charge of it. Once you share it, it is out of your control, and it may hurt you.

IN THE SOURCES

A rebuke enters deeper into a man of understanding than a hundred lashes into a fool. (Mishlei 17:10)

Physical suffering is better than shame. (Sotah 8b)

WORDS OF OUR SAGES

Wounds heal, but not harsh words.
(R' Yosef Kimchi on Mishlei)

אַ פּאַטש פאַרגייט, אַ וואָרט באַשטייט.

A patsh fargeit, a vort bashteit.

A harsh word lasts longer than a slap.

MEANING

Be very careful when using words; their mark is on the spirit, their effect long-lasting.

דעם וועלטס מויל קען מען נישט פֿאַרשפּאַרן.

Dem velt's moil ken men nisht farshparren.

You can't lock the world's mouth.

METAPHORICAL MEANING
Once people have begun talking about something, it is impossible to control its dissemination.

הערן און זען און...שווייַגן.

Heren un zehn un...shveigen.

Hear, see, and...be silent.

MEANING
Keep your eyes and ears open, but your mouth shut.

IN THE SOURCES
...and Mishma, and Dumah, and Massa [names of Ishmael's sons].
(Bereshis 25:14)

[The words mean:] Listen, be silent, and think.
(Targum Yonasan ibid.)

Hear, be silent, and bear it.
(Rambam, Iggeres Teiman)

אַ גוט וואָרט געפֿינט זיך אַן אָרט.

A gut vort gefint zich an ort.

A good word finds its place. (A kind word is never lost.)

MEANING
A good word is never redundant.

IN THE SOURCES
There is nothing (davar/dibbur) that has no place. (Avos 4:3)

IN THE SOURCES
Death and life are in the power of the tongue.
(Mishlei 18:21)

די גאנצע וועלט שטייט אויף דעם שפיץ צונג.

Di gantzeh velt shteit oif dem shpitz tzung.

The whole world rests on the tip of the tongue (on the spoken word).

METAPHORICAL MEANING
You may use the "tip of your tongue" – a question – to find out about anywhere in the world.

נישט געזאָגט איז אויך געזאָגט.

Nisht gezogt iz oich gezogt.

No response is also a response.

MEANING
Silence speaks volumes.

IN TALES OF THE CHASIDIM
R' Menachem Mendel of Kotzk related the following:

When the "Holy Yid" lay dying, Chasidim cried bitterly and recited Psalms with a great emotional outpouring. I, however, stood silently next to the furnace, neither moving nor uttering a sound.

R' Simcha Bunim of Przysucha approached me and said: "Menachem Mendel, why are you causing such a commotion in the cosmos?!"

אַ װאָרט איז װי אַ פֿײַל; בײדע האָבן גרױס געאײַל.

A vort iz vi a feil; beideh hoben grois ge'eil.

A word is like an arrow;
both are in a hurry to strike.

INSTRUCTION
Be careful how you use words!

IN THE SOURCES
"With my sword and my bow." – My prayer and my supplication. (Bereshis 48:22)

Their tongue is a sharpened arrow. (Yirmeyahu 9:7)

And they bend their tongue, their bow... (Ibid. 9:2)

As a maul, and a sword, and a sharp arrow – so is a man who bears false witness against his neighbor. (Mishlei 25:18)

פֿון שװײַגן האָט מען קײן חרטה נישט.

Fun shveigen hot men kein charoteh nisht.

You won't be sorry for being silent.

IN TALES OF THE CHASIDIM
A shochet (ritual slaughterer) approached R' Eisel Charif with the following problem:
Someone had suggested a match for his daughter with a young God-fearing scholar who maintained an extreme degree of silence.
Said R' Eisel: "Not every slaughter of the shochet is kosher, but every silence of a silent one is good!"

IN THE SOURCES
A word is worth a sela; silence is worth two. (Megillah 18a)

All my days I grew up among scholars and have found nothing better for oneself than silence. (Avos 1:17)

A fence for wisdom is silence. (Ibid. 3:13)

WORDS OF OUR SAGES
*If sometime you regret being silent – you will regret many times your having spoken.
(Rabbi Shlomo ben Gabirol)*

עס איז נישטאָ קיין גלײַכערס
ווי אַ קרומער לייטער,
און עס איז נישטאָ קיין קרומערס
ווי אַ גלײַכווערטל.

(R' Naftali of Ropshitz)

*Es iz nishto kein gleichers vi a krumer leiter,
un es iz nishto kein krumers vi a gleichvertel.*

There is nothing so straight as a crooked ladder, and nothing so crooked as a direct insult.

MEANING
Some things are better when they are not straight, enabling one to more easily reach one's goal, such as a ladder, that can be climbed only when it is "crooked" – leaning. On the other hand, there are things whose straightness causes their user to deviate from the true path, such as "straight talk" that insults and causes inevitable damage. Thus "straight" and "crooked" are relative terms, to be judged on their merits...

IN TALES OF THE CHASIDIM
R' Naftali of Ropshitz was known for his sharp, keen statements. Before his passing, he said: "I am proud of having never uttered an insulting word."

B. TRUTH AND FALSEHOOD

אַ ליגן טאָר מען נישט זאָגן;
דעם אמת מוז מען נישט זאָגן.

*A liggen tor men nisht zoggen;
dem emes muz men nisht zoggen.*

A lie you *must* not tell; the truth you *need* not tell.

MEANING
An admonition to those who pass on harmful information; one must weigh the potential harm that even the truth can cause, when shared at the wrong time and place.

IN THE SOURCES
Distance yourself from falsehood. (Shemos 23:7)

WORDS OF OUR SAGES
He who spreads gossip about another commits a sin...although it may be the truth. The same applies to one who denigrates one's fellow – even if what is said is true.
(Chafetz Chaim, Lavin;1)

אַז מ'זאָגט דעם אמת —
פאַרשפּאָרט מען צו שווערן.

Az m'zogt dem emes – farshport men tzu shveren.

One who admits the truth need not swear to it.

MEANING
It is best to admit the truth, though it may be painful, and thus avoid further complications.

IN THE SOURCES
He who makes a partial admission to a claim against him must take an oath. (He who makes a full admission, however, need not swear.) (Bava Kama 107a)

IN THE SOURCES

[The spies said:] "We came to the land...and indeed it flows with milk and honey...however..."
(Bemidbar 13:27) –
A lie cannot endure unless it begins with some truth.
(Rashi)

WORDS OF OUR SAGES

A sick person who lies to the doctor cheats only himself, wastes the doctor's time, and aggravates his own illness. (Rabbenu Bachya)

You must not let embarrassment prevent you from sharing with your religious mentor all your thoughts that are inconsistent with our holy Torah.
(R' Elimelech of Lizhensk)

אַ האַלבער אמת
איז אַ גאַנצער ליגן.

A halber emes iz a gantzer liggen.

A half-truth is a whole lie.

MEANING
Half the truth is as misleading as a lie.

פאַר דרײַ זאָגט מען דעם אמת:
פאַרן דאָקטער, פאַרן אַדוואָקאַט,
און פאַרן רבין.

*Far drei zogt men dem emes:
farn dokter, farn advokat, un farn rebbin.*

One tells the truth to three people: the doctor, the lawyer, and the rabbi.

MEANING
It is necessary to share the truth with those who are expected to help treat one's problems.

Every Word Counts

מיט ליגן קומט מען אָן ווײַט,
אָבער נישט צוריק.

*Mit liggen kumt men on veit,
ober nisht tzurik.*

With lies you may go far, but not come back.
(Lies have short wings.)

MEANING
This is a warning against lying: The liar believes it will help him, but, in truth, the damage it causes is irreversible!

IN THE SOURCES
Distance yourself from falsehood. (Shemos 23:7)

Facetiously: Because of falsehood, you will go far.

אויף אַ מעשׂה
פֿרעגט מען נישט קיין קשיא.

Oif a maaseh fregt men nisht kein kasheh.

Don't question facts.

MEANING
You can't argue with the facts, because they are more convincing than any hypothesis.

Alternative meaning: The word "maaseh" means "fact" or "story."

Don't question a story.

MEANING
It does not pay to question the logic of an anecdote or fiction, for in them anything is possible.

WORDS OF OUR SAGES
*Words are believed less than actions. (Abarbanel)
(Or: Actions speak louder than words.)*

IN THE SOURCES
Fear what the world fears.
(Yerushalmi Terumos 8:3)

אַז די וועלט זאָגט זאָל מען גלייבן.

Az di velt zogt zol men gleiben.

If everyone says so, there must be some truth to it.

IN TALES OF THE CHASIDIM

On the verse *(Bereshis 29:17)*, "And Leah's eyes were weak," Rashi comments: She cried because she thought she was destined to [marry] Esav, for everyone was saying, "Rivkah has two sons and Lavan has two daughters; the elder will marry the elder and the younger, the younger."

R' Menachem Mendel of Kotzk asked: "Who was 'everyone'? – Lavan and his boorish, unthinking shepherds. Did Leah believe such liars!?" This teaches us that one must take seriously what people say!

*   *   *

There was a disagreement between R' Meir of Kretchnif and his attendant: The rabbi claimed that it was possible to fool people concerning one's actual status, while his attendant disagreed. The rabbi proposed that they exchange clothes and travel to a place where they were unknown, to see how they would be treated. They came to a small town, where word soon spread that the Rabbi of Kretchnif – of whom the inhabitants had heard much – had arrived. Young and old, the townsfolk gathered to bask in the tzaddik's radiance and to receive his blessing. The town's richest man invited the two to be his guests. He prepared a sumptuous meal to which he also invited some of the rabbi's well-wishers. The "attendant," too, pitched in enthusiastically to help his host properly serve the "rabbi."

During the meal, the "attendant" noticed that the guests were whispering to each other while staring at the "rabbi" and his "attendant." The rich host kept staring at them as well. He eventually turned to R' Meir and whispered to him: "Pardon me, Sir, for intruding into something that is not my business, and perhaps I am mistaken, but in my view, and that of many of those present, it appears that you are more worthy of being rabbi than he whom you are serving."

R' Meir smiled upon realizing that his attendant had been right; people are, indeed, perceptive.

אַזוי ווי איך הָאָב געקויפט, אַזוי פֿאַרקויף איך.

Azoi vi ich hob gekoift, azoi farkoif ich.

As I bought it, so I am selling it.

METAPHORICAL MEANING
A response to mistrust of something said. Alternatively, it denies responsibility for what was said: "I am merely passing on exactly what I heard."

נישט געשטויגן נישט געפֿלויגן.

Nisht geshtoigen nisht gefloigen.

It neither took off nor flew.

METAPHORICAL MEANING
A description of something that had never been based in reality.

IN THE SOURCES
Never was nor created.
(Bava Basra 15a)

There was neither a forest nor were there bears.
(Sotah 47a)

די מעשה האָט שוין אַ לאַנגע באָרד; יעדער לייגט צו אַ האָר.

Di maaseh hot shoin a langeh bord; yeder leigt tzu a hor.

The story already has a long beard; everyone adds a hair to it.

METAPHORICAL MEANING

This is a response to hearing a familiar story (or joke), to which changes or additions have been made by its many and varied narrators.

IN THE SOURCES

Falsehood has no legs.
(Rashi to Mishlei 12:22; Tikkunei Zohar 22)

And truth is lacking.
(Yeshayahu 59:15)

דער שקר האָט נישט קיין פּים, איז ער געבליבן; דער אמת האָט פּים, איז ער אַנטלאָפֿן.

Der shekker hot nisht kein fis, iz er geblibben; der emes hot fis, iz er antloffen.

A lie has no feet, so it remains; truth has feet, so it runs away.

EXPLANATION

This ironic proverb is patterned on a rabbinical saying found in the Sources. Its somber conclusion is apparently based on reality: Falsehood exists in everything, while truth is elusive.

C. PRAISES, WISHES, AND BLESSINGS

עס איז איבער אים אַ ברכה צו מאַכן.

Es iz ibber im a brocheh tzu machen.

One should say a blessing over him/it.

MEANING
An expression of admiration upon seeing someone or something.

> **IN THE SOURCES**
> Upon seeing beautiful creatures, one says: Blessed is He Whose world contains such things. (Berachos 58b)
>
> Upon seeing a beautiful marble pillar, a person should say: Blessed is the quarry from which the beautiful world was quarried, and blessed is the One Who created and quarried this.
> (Shemos Rabbah 15:22)

מ'דאַרף ראוי זיין די ברכה זאָל מקויים ווערן.

M'darf ro'uy zein di brocheh zol mekuyem verren.

May we deserve that the blessing come true.

MEANING
The humble response of one who has received a blessing: According to the merits of the one bestowing the blessing, it deserves to take effect. May I, however, be worthy of receiving it!

> **IN THE SOURCES**
> If he is deserving, it will be for him as a healing drug. If not, it will become a deadly poison for him. (Yoma 72b)
>
> I have acted evilly and ruined my livelihood.
> (Kiddushin 72b)

זאָלסט האָבן אסתר-המלכה'ס חן.

Zolst hobben Esther-Hamalkeh's chein.

May you have Queen Esther's grace.

MEANING
A wish that one find favor in others' eyes.

IN THE SOURCES
And Esther found favor in the sight of all who looked upon her. (Esther 2:15)

זאָלסט האָבן שלמה-המלך'ס חכמה און קורח'ס אוצר.

Zolst hobben Shlomeh-Hamelech's chochmeh un Korach's otzar.

May you have King Solomon's wisdom and Korach's wealth.

MEANING
A wish for wisdom and riches.

IN THE SOURCES
And God said [to Solomon]:... "I have given you a wise and understanding heart, so that there has been none like you before you, neither shall any arise like you after you." (Melachim I 3:11-12)

This is the wealth of Korach, for he was richer than anyone else in Israel. (Shemos Rabbah 31:2)

פֿון דײַן מויל אין גאָט'ס אויערן

Fun dein moil in Gott's oiern

From your mouth to God's ears

MEANING
A response and agreement to one's wish: May your wish be acceptable to the One Who is able to carry it out!

IN THE SOURCES
O my God, incline Your ear and hear. (Daniel 9:18)

I love...because He has inclined His ear unto me. (Tehillim 116:1-2)

מ׳זאל זיך אָפּדינען אין פֿריידן.

M'zol zich ofdinnen in freiden.

May we reciprocate on your happy occasions.

MEANING
This is a response to a good deed: May only good come to you, so that we shall be able to repay your kindness only at joyous occasions.

וואו דו וועסט זיין, און צו וואס דו וועסט זיך קערן, זאל דיר גאט געבן א רווח מיט א קרן!

Vu du vest zein, un tzu vos du vest zich kerren, zol dir Gott geben a revach mit a keren!

In whatever you do, and wherever you turn, may God grant you principal with interest!

EXPLANATION
A person must exert himself to build up capital. Interest is profit that is obtained without additional effort.

MEANING
A wish that one may be blessed with returns above and beyond one's investment.

IN THE SOURCES
Hashem, the God of your fathers, will make you a thousand times as many as you are, and bless you, as He has promised you.
(Devarim 1:11)

אִיז עֶס פֿון כרײן, זאָל עֶס צוגײן;
אִיז דאָס פֿון מערן, זאָל דאָס צושלערן.

Iz es fun chrein, zol es tzugein;
iz dos fun merren, zol dos tzushlerren.

If it's bitter like horseradish, may it dissipate; if it's sweet like a carrot, may it bind.

MEANING
This is a wish concerning a proposed match, or any other venture, whose quality is as yet unknown.
If it's good for me, let it develop; if not, may it become null and void.

IN THE SOURCES
God watches over the simple. (Tehillim 116:6)

God protects those who are incapable of knowing about and protecting themselves from danger.
(Responsa Shevet Mi-Yehudah 1:19)

אַזוי ווי ער ווייסט נישט,
אַזוי זאָל דאָס אים נישט שאַדן.

Azoi vi er veist nisht,
azoi zol dos im nisht shadden.

What he doesn't know shouldn't hurt him.

MEANING
Reaction to an action fraught with danger, performed innocently.

D. ENCOURAGING WORDS FOR THE SUFFERING AND THE NEEDY

וואו עם וואקסן דערנער דארט וועט וואקסן אַ רויז.

Vu es vaksen derner dort vet vaksen a roiz.

Where thorns grow, there will grow a rose.

METAPHORICAL MEANING
Trials and tribulations provide fertile ground for the growth of one's soul.

IN THE SOURCES
As a rose among thorns, so is my beloved among the daughters.
(Shir Ha-Shirim 2:2)

Be careful with the children of the poor, for from them shall Torah emerge.
(Nedarim 81a)

WORDS OF OUR SAGES
A pearl must have a stony shell; grain must have chaff; a vineyard must have weeds; and a rose must have thorns.
(R' Yaakov Emden)

אין יעדער אומגליק איז דאָ אַ גליק.

In yeder umglick iz do a glick.

In every misfortune there is [buried good] fortune.

EXPLANATION
The Yiddish contains a play on words: the word "glick" is "buried" in the word "umglick."

MEANING
Encouraging words for anyone in sorrow: God aims to bestow goodness upon His creatures. Therefore, even if something that happens seems to be bad, it is merely a covering for good that will grow out of it.

WORDS OF OUR SAGES
We must have faith that troubles are like the decaying of the seed, which is followed by growth.
(Esh Dos – Ozerov)

In every bad there is good; in every judgment, kindness.
(R' Dov Ber of Mezritch)

ס'איז שוין נענטער ווי ווײַטער.

S'iz shoin nenter vi veiter.

It's already closer than further.

MEANING

Encouragement to someone who is impatient about reaching his destination: You have already invested most of the required energy; all you have to do is to complete the effort in order to benefit from its fruits!

פֿאַרוואָס ביסטו צוגעלייגט? דיינע קאַטשקעס דרייען זיך אַרום באָרוועס?

Farvos bistu tzugeleigt?
Deineh katshkes dreien zich arum borvess?

Why are you so upset? Are your ducks walking around barefoot?

EXPLANATION

It is normal for ducks to be barefoot; it is good for them, and there is no need to worry about it.

METAPHORICAL MEANING

Comforting words for the worrier: Everything is as it should be, so there is no reason for you to worry!

גוטע זאַכן קומען אומגעריכט.

Guteh zachen kummen umgericht.

Good things come without warning.

MEANING
Encouragement to one who is in despair: Hope for good even when it is unexpected.

IN THE SOURCES
Three appear without warning: the messiah, a found object, and a scorpion. (Sanhedrin 97a)

די גאַנצע וועלט איז נישט ווערד אַ קרעכץ, אָבער אַז ס'טוט וויי שרײַט מען.

Di gantzeh velt iz nisht verd a krechtz, obber az s'tut vei shreit men.

The whole world is not worth a groan, but when it hurts we cry out.

MEANING
An expression of sympathy for one who cries out due to the hardships that have befallen him: In truth the world is not worth a moan, but man is influenced by his physical nature, and it is therefore difficult for him to hold back from crying out when in pain.

WORDS OF OUR SAGES
The entire world is not worth even one sigh.
(Rabbi Menachem Mendel of Kotzk)

IN THE SOURCES
There is comfort to be found in the affliction of the many.
(Ha-Chinuch, Mitzvah 331)

WORDS OF OUR SAGES
Join the community, because the wolf will snatch the sheep that wanders off alone. (R' Moshe ben Ezra)

וואָס עס וועט זיַין מיט כלל ישׂראל וועט זיַין מיט ר' ישׂראל.

Vos es vet zein mit Klal Yisroel vet zein mit Reb Yisroel.

What will happen with all Israel will happen to Mr. Israel.

MEANING
A saying that attempts to calm one who is worried about the future: An individual's destiny is bound up with that of society.

IN TALES OF THE CHASIDIM
R' Yaakov of Polnaah told the following parable:

Once a great and powerful king led his army in besieging a fortified city. First, the strong and courageous soldiers stormed the wall and breached it. They were followed by regular soldiers who entered through the breaches and captured positions. The weaker soldiers trailed along, contributing almost nothing... When the city was captured, however, everyone burst in as one, and began pillaging and dividing up the spoils, without discrimination.

The same may be applied to us: The lowly and weak among the Jewish people enjoy the fruits of the merits of their great leaders' work.

ערגער ווי ערגער
קען דאָך שוין נישט זיַין.

Erger vi erger ken doch shoin nisht zein.

It can't be worse than it already is.

MEANING
Encouragement to the fallen: Since you have reached the bottom level, you can't fall any further, so the only option you have is to go up.

IN TALES OF THE CHASIDIM
There came to Rabbi Yisrael of Sadigora a Jew who had once been very wealthy, but had become progressively poorer, until he was destitute.
The rabbi said to him: Now that you have reached the lowliest state, I am certain that your salvation is near and that you will regain your previous stature, for man's fortune is like a turning spoked wheel. Upon reaching the top of the wheel, the uppermost spoke begins to descend, doing so until it reaches the bottom of the wheel, from where it can turn nowhere else but upwards.

WORDS OF CHASIDIM
One cannot fall from the ground.

MAMMA USED TO SAY

> **IN THE SOURCES**
> *Poverty is as becoming to a Jew as a red ribbon to a white horse.* (Chagigah 9b)

אָרעם איז קיין שַאנד.

Orem iz kein shand.

To be poor is not disgraceful.

MEANING

A saying meant to uplift the poor: Poverty is decreed on man by heaven in order to bring him toward his purpose in life. It does not attest to one's worthlessness, so that it is nothing of which to be ashamed.

IN TALES OF THE CHASIDIM

R' Yissachar Dov Horowitz brought a nice garment to R' Yaakov Aryeh of Radzimin, when the latter was going through a difficult period, and said to him: "Going around in tattered clothes as a pauper is disgraceful."

R' Aryeh responded: "With my poverty, a gift from God, I should be embarrassed, but with clothing, a gift of man, I should be proud!?"

> **IN THE SOURCES**
> *People hate the poor, no one loves the poor, and the poor person's wisdom is not heeded.*
> (Osios d'Rabbi Akiva 2:4)

ארעם איז קיין שאַנד, אָבער אויך קיין כבוד נישט.

Orem iz kein shand, ober oich kein kovod nisht.

It's no shame to be poor – but it's no great honor either.

MEANING

This relates to the previous saying, but contains a mild rebuke for those who boast of being poor.

A Time for Everything

A TIME FOR EVERYTHING

A. HOW MAN USES AND IS INFLUENCED BY TIME

לייג נישט אָפּ אויף מאָרגן וואָס דו קענסט היינט באַזאָרגן.

*Leig nisht op oif morgen
vos du kenst heint bazorgen.*

Don't put off till tomorrow what you can do today.

MEANING
A saying meant for people who tend to make excuses for postponing tasks.

IN THE SOURCES
Don't say, "When I have free time, I'll study," for you may not have free time. (Avos 2:14)

Repent today, lest you die tomorrow. (Shabbos 153)

WORDS OF OUR SAGES
"...and go out, fight with Amalek; tomorrow..." – there is an Amalek called "tomorrow"...
(Chasidic saying)

"And [Jacob] blessed them that day, saying..." (Bereshis 48:20) – He blessed them that they should say, "On that day – [meaning:] I will do it today and not tomorrow."
(R' Asher of Karlin)

זוך נישט דעם נעכטיקן טאָג.

Zuch nisht dem nechtiken tog.

Don't look for yesterday.

METAPHORICAL MEANING
Don't look for something that was and is no more; live the present and look to the future.

IN THE SOURCES
...as yesterday when it is past. (Tehillim 90:4)

What was, was; we'll begin the account from now onward. (Vayikra Rabbah 30:7)

דאָס נעכטיקע מאָרגן איז הײַנט.

Dos nechtikeh morgen iz heint.

The "tomorrow" of yesterday is today.

MEANING

An expression of dissatisfaction with the tendency to push things off until "tomorrow."

INSTRUCTION

Enough procrastination! Get up and do today what yesterday you put off until "tomorrow."

מאָרגן איז אויך אַ טאָג.

Morgen iz oich a tog.

Tomorrow is also a day.
(Tomorrow is another day.)

MEANING

Wait for tomorrow (for example, if you could not get something accomplished today); perhaps new possibilities and opportunities will become available then that were not present today.

A Time for Everything

אַ ליידיק גייער
האָט קיין מאָל קיין צייט נישט.

A leidik geier hot kein mol kein tzeit nisht.

An idle person never has time.

MEANING

People who make good use of their time find spare time when they need it. Idlers, who waste their time, have great difficulty finding any free time.

אַ פֿאַרנומענער מענטש
האָט שטענדיק צייט.

A farnumener mentsh hot shtendik tzeit.

A busy person always has time.

MEANING

A person who knows the value of time spends it appropriately. He will therefore always find time for important purposes.

WORDS OF OUR SAGES

"And I will pay attention [ופניתי] to you" (Vayikra 26:9) – This is related to the word פנאי, free time. Every servant of God, whoever clings to Him, has spare time for everything.
(Chiddushei Ha-Rim)

IN THE SOURCES

And the sun stayed in the midst of heaven, and hasted not to go down about a whole day. (Yehoshua 10:13)

נאָר איין מאָל
איז די זון שטיין געבליבן.

Nor ein mol iz di zun shtein geblibben.

Only once did the sun stand still.

INSTRUCTION

Hurry, time is being lost! Chances are nil that you will see time stand still again.

ס'געהערט נישט צום נעכטן
און נישט צום מאָרגן.

*S'gehert nisht tzum nechten
un nisht tzum morgen.*

It is neither of yesterday,
nor of tomorrow.

METAPHORICAL MEANING

A description of an event, person, or thing that is removed from reality.

אַז מ'וואַרט, דערוואַרט מען זיך.

Az m'vart, dervart men zich.

He who waits [patiently] will attain [his goal].

MEANING
It is sometimes worthwhile to wait patiently.

IN THE SOURCES
Haste makes waste.
(Pesachim 50b)

WORDS OF OUR SAGES
Patience has its rewards.
(R' Moshe ben Ezra)

Man will attain much more by being patient than he will by all the determination in the world.
(Gaon of Vilna)

אַ יאָר מיט אַ מיטוואָך

A yor mit a Mitvoch

A year and a Wednesday

EXPLANATION
A year, plus a few days until the first Wednesday that follows – This was the maximum period of time a bride had, between her betrothal and wedding, to prepare her trousseau.

METAPHORICAL MEANING
An expression that alludes to the fact that the maximum period of time that was needed for a certain project has already been allocated.

IN THE SOURCES
A maiden is allotted twelve months. *(Kesubos 57a)*

A maiden gets married on Wednesday. *(Ibid. 2a)*

B. THE SYMBOLISM OF FESTIVALS AND OTHER OCCASIONS

אַ יום-טוב אין דער וואָכנס
A Yom-Tov in der vochens

A holiday in the middle of the week

METAPHORICAL MEANING
A description of and reaction to inappropriate festive behavior.

IN TALES OF THE CHASIDIM
R' Yisrael of Ruzhin had a policy in his home that his children might never enter his room on weekdays, only on Sabbaths and festivals.

Once his precocious little son Avraham Yitzchak (later the Elder Rebbe of Sadigora) entered his father's special room on a weekday.

His father turned to him and asked, "Have you made yourself a holiday in the middle of the week?"

"When I see Daddy it's a holiday for me!" said the child. This earned him his righteous father's blessing: "They shall not be removed from your mouth."

A Time for Everything

אַ גאַנז טאָר פּרשת-זכור נישט
הערן; אַ אינדיק — "עבדים היינו";
אַ הון — אַ קול שופר.

A ganz tor Parshas-Zochor nisht heren;
a indik — "Avodim Hoyinu";
a hun — a kol shofar.

Don't let a goose hear Parashas-Zachor, a turkey "Avadim Hayinu," and a rooster the sounding of the shofar.

EXPLANATION
Don't let a goose hear Parashas-Zachor, which heralds its being slaughtered for the upcoming festive Purim meal. Don't let a turkey hear "Avadim Hayinu," which is recited on the Shabbos preceding Passover, the festival on which it will be eaten. Nor is it good for the rooster to hear the shofar on Rosh Hashanah, for it carries the message that the rooster will soon be slaughtered for Kaparos.

METAPHORICAL MEANING
If you wish to catch someone, don't tell him about the danger awaiting him.

IN THE SOURCES
See how God's behavior differs from that of human beings: A person who wishes to inflict harm on another tries to hide it from him. God, however, acts differently: He sends a warning; perhaps the person will repent and be spared.
(Midrash Ha-Gadol, Noach)

אַ אידישער זומער: זיבן ציילט מען,
דרײַ וויינט מען, פיר בלאָזט מען,
און דער זומער איז אַוועק.

*A Yiddisher zummer: ziben tzeilt men,
drei veint men, fier blozt men,
un der zummer iz avek.*

A Jewish summer: we count seven, we cry three, we blow four, and the summer is gone.

MEANING

The Jewish summer is special in that it, too, is steeped in holiness; it is not a time for lightheartedness or slacking. It begins with the seven weeks of counting the Omer, a time of customary sorrow, which is followed by "the three weeks" of mourning, and ends with the four weeks of the month of Elul, the awesome period preceding the days of judgment during which the shofar is sounded.

געקומען מיט די פּסח'דיקע געפעס.

Gekummen mit di Pesach'dikeh gefess.

He arrived with Passover utensils.

METAPHORICAL MEANING

He brought his household with him. This is a statement that is critical of anyone who unnecessarily drags along with him people, utensils, or other objects.

מ'פֿאַשעט די גאַנץ אַ גאַנץ יאָר; ס'קומט פּסח איז זי טרייף.

*M'pashet di ganz a gantz yor;
s'kumt Pesach iz zi treif.*

You stuff the goose all year long, but when Passover arrives it is "treif."

EXPLANATION
East European Jews used to fatten geese in order to honor the Passover holiday with their meat and fat.

METAPHORICAL MEANING
Much work was invested, with disappointing results.

IN THE SOURCES
Clouds and wind without rain. (Mishlei 25:14)

Planting among thorns. (Yirmeyahu 4:3)

מ'האָט צו דערציילן ווי בײַ יציאת מצרים.

*M'hot tzu dertzeilen
vi bei Yetzias Mitzrayim.*

There's a lot to tell – like about the Exodus.

METAPHORICAL MEANING
It's a long story, and it has many lessons for us.

IN THE SOURCES
And whoever expounds the Exodus at length is praiseworthy. (Passover Haggadah)

IN THE SOURCES
And it shall be when your son in the future asks...
(Shemos 13:14)

טאָמער איז בײַ אידן שוין יאָ אַמאָל אַ סדר, פרעגט מען "מה נשתנה."

Tommer iz bei Yidden shoin yo amol a seder, fregt men "Mah Nishtanah."

When a Jew manages to make a Seder, "Mah Nishtanah [why is this night different?]" will be asked.

METAPHORICAL MEANING
Reply to a scornful reaction to someone who has met with unexpected success.

IN TALES OF THE CHASIDIM
When R' Yehonasan Eibeschutz was a child, his father asked him at the Seder: "Could you explain why Jewish children ask "Mah Nishtanah" on Pesach, rather than on Sukkos when they see everyone leave their home and go out to live in sukkahs for eight days?!"

Little Yehonasan answered: "On Sukkos the children are not surprised to see their people sitting in a poor sukkah, because the Jewish people are used to having trouble and hard times. On the other hand, during the Seder night, when everyone sits around like kings, children stare at the unusual sight and blurt out "Why is this night different?"

דעם אָרעמאַן איז גרינג
אַרויסצורוימען דעם חמץ,
און שווער אַריינצוברענגען
דעם פּסח.

*Dem oremann iz gring
aroistzuroimen dem chometz,
un shver areintzubrengen dem Pesach.*

It's easy for the poor man
to get rid of his chametz,
but difficult for him to bring in
the Passover.

MEANING
A description that illustrates the poor man's distress: his house is empty, and he has nothing with which to fill it.

IN JEWISH FOLKLORE
One of the town's poor proclaimed on the day before Passover that he was already able to fulfill half the festival's commandments – that of "no chametz shall be seen with you." The other half, however – "you shall eat matzah seven days" – he was not yet able to fulfill.

IN THE SOURCES
...but the poor man had nothing. (Shemuel II, 12:3)

עס דויערט
פֿון תּענית אסתּר ביז פּורים.

Es doiert fun Taanis Esther biz Purim.

It will last from the Fast of Esther until Purim.

EXPLANATION

There is no time at all between the Fast of Esther and Purim, because Purim begins when the Fast of Esther ends.

METAPHORICAL MEANING

The article or agreement won't last.

ער גייט אַרום
ווי אַ שוחט אין די ניין טעג.

Er geit arum vi a shochet in di nein teg.

He walks around like a slaughterer during the Nine Days.

EXPLANATION

It is forbidden to eat meat during the first nine days of the month of Av. Ritual slaughterers are therefore idle then.

METAPHORICAL MEANING

A description of someone who acts as if he has nothing to do.

ראש חודש אלול ציטערט אפילו אַ פיש אין וואַסער.

Rosh Chodesh Elul tzittert afilu a fish in vasser.

Even fish in water tremble at the arrival of the Days of Awe.

MEANING
A description of the fear of judgment that grips all creatures during the period when the world is judged.

ווי אַ האָן אין "בני אדם"

Vi a hon in "b'nei odom"

As a rooster in "b'nei adam" [people]

EXPLANATION
When the Kaparos ritual is performed on Erev Yom Kippur, the following verse is recited: "People who sit in darkness and in the shadow of death..." *(Tehillim 107:10)*. It is said while one holds the "atonement rooster" in one hand and the prayer book in the other. The rooster, being near the prayer book, appears to be reading and understanding the text, whence the saying has arisen.

METAPHORICAL MEANING
A description of someone who is trying to understand something that is way above him.

IN THE SOURCES

Fear and trembling will grip them...when You remember and consider the soul of all living beings; there are many deeds and an infinite number of creatures to be remembered...
(Musaf for Rosh Hashanah)

MAMMA USED TO SAY

IN THE SOURCES
This is what he said: "Please, God, I have sinned...." This is how he counted: "One, one and one...."
(from the Yom Kippur Musaf prayer)

אַ גרויסער חילוק פון "וכך היה אומר" ביז "וכך היה מונה."

A groisser chiluk fun "v'chach hoyoh omer" biz "v'chach hoyoh moneh."

There's a great distance between "this is what he said" and "this is how he counted."

EXPLANATION
In the Musaf prayer service of Yom Kippur, we say in the section that describes the High Priest's service on that day, "This is what he said...." The description continues, as we recite the words and bow down, until we reach, "This is how he counted...."

METAPHORICAL MEANING
It's a long way from the promise to contribute money – "This is what he said" – to its fulfillment: "This is how he counted."

IN THE SOURCES
Pity one who has no home, but makes a gate for a home.
(Shabbos 31b)

אַז מ'האָט נישט קיין אתרוג דאַרף מען קיין פושקע נישט האָבן.

Az m'hot nisht kein esrog darf men kein pushkeh nisht hobben.

When you don't have an esrog, you don't need a box for it.

METAPHORICAL MEANING
When the main article is absent, its accessories are superfluous.

ס'געיט אים מיט דעם פיטם אַראָפּ.

S'geit im mit di pittem arop.

His esrog fell with the tip down.

EXPLANATION
When an esrog (citron, a fruit used ritually on Sukkos) falls on its tip, it almost certainly becomes unfit.

METAPHORICAL MEANING
He is having bad luck.

ער זעט אוים ווי אַ אָפּגעשלאָגענע הושענא.

Er zet ois vi a opgeshloggeneh hoshana.

He looks like a beaten hoshana (bundle of five willow twigs).

EXPLANATION
The prophets Chaggai, Zechariah, and Malachi established the taking up of willows on the last day of Sukkos (Hoshana Rabbah), reciting a prayer over them and then beating them five times on the floor.

METAPHORICAL MEANING
He looks wretched and beaten, like the willow twigs after they have been struck on Hoshana Rabbah.

IN THE SOURCES

God grants one an extra soul on the eve of the Sabbath, and takes it away on Saturday night, as it is written, "שבת וינפש" (shavas vayinafash, "He rested and was refreshed," Shemos 31:17).
The Gemara comments: After he rested (שבת shavas), vay (וי alas), he lost a soul (נפש nefesh).
(Beitzah 16a)

One must be careful to refrain from talking about light matters after the Sabbath and holy days, because one can suddenly fall from a high roof into a deep hole. (Midrash Pinchas)

נאָך אַ יום-טוב בלייבט מען
מיט דרײַ זאכען:
אַ בײזן האַלז,
אַ ליידיקע קעשענע,
און אַ פולן זאַק
מיט ברודיקע וועש.

Noch a Yom-Tov bleibt men mit drei zachen: a beizen halz, a leidikeh keshenneh, un a fullen zack mit brudikkeh vesh.

Three things remain after a holiday: an angry throat, an empty pocket, and a sack full of dirty clothes.

MEANING

The Jewish soul feels lacking following its fall from the sanctity of a holy day to a weekday. The Jew expresses this sense of loss by referring to the accompanying physical discomforts.

By the Sweat of Your Brow

BY THE SWEAT OF YOUR BROW
MONEY, TRADE, AND LIVELIHOOD

"געלט" איז "בלאָטע."

"Gelt" iz "blotteh."

Money is like mud.

EXPLANATION
The saying is a reference to the comparison between one who is sinking into a monetary quagmire and one who is sinking in mud. It is also a reference to the numerical equivalence (gematriya) of געלט and בלאטע ("money" and "mud" equal 112).

METAPHORICAL MEANING
An expression of contempt for money: Money causes one who immerses himself in it to sink into materialism.

IN THE SOURCES
How do we know that money (כסף) is synonymous with shame? – Because Aramaic for "shame" is כסופא. (Bemidbar Rabbah 14:22)

WORDS OF OUR SAGES
Why is it called a coin (מטבע)? – Because one sinks (טובע) in it.
(R' Avraham of Slonim)

אַ שווערער בײַטל מאַכט אַ לײַכט געמיט.

A shverer beitel macht a leicht gemiet.

A heavy purse makes life easier.

METAPHORICAL MEANING
A saying that underscores the importance of money in one's life.

IN THE SOURCES
The heart is suspended in a pouch (or: hangs/depends on a pocket).
(Yerushalmi Terumos 5:4)

Three sounds gladden the heart: The sound of money, the sound of Torah, and the sound of rain.
(Otzar Midrashim, p. 168)

IN THE SOURCES
Money covers up shame.
(Based on Ma'avar Yabok)

WORDS OF OUR SAGES
Man's wealth hides his blemishes and straightens his crookedness.
(R' Shlomo ben Gevirol)

מיט געלט פארשטאפט מען דער וועלט דאָס מויל.

Mit gelt farshtopt men der velt dos moil.

Money makes the world keep its mouth shut.

METAPHORICAL MEANING
Money puts one in a position of strength that makes others refrain from discussing his faults.

IN THE SOURCES
Money answers all things.
(Koheles 10:19)

געלט פארענטפערט אלע קשיות.

Gelt farentfert alleh kashyos.

Money solves all problems. (Money talks.)

METAPHORICAL MEANING
Money settles complaints and gets rid of obstacles.

IN THE SOURCES
Whoever is plagued with poverty is as if he has all the problems in the world.
(Shemos Rabbah 31:14)

אָן געלט איז קיין וועלט.

On gelt iz kein velt.

Without money, no world. (No dough, no go!)

MEANING
One's world is incomplete without money.

געלט איז גאָרנישט; האָסטו נישט קיין געלט – ביסטו גאָרנישט!

Gelt iz gornisht; hostu nisht kein gelt – bistu gornisht!

Money is nothing; without money, you are nothing!

MEANING

A saying that expresses man's ambivalence toward money: Money itself is not a value, but with it one can realize one's desires and aspirations. Therefore, one who lacks money lacks power, and his value is diminished in the eyes of others.

IN THE SOURCES
A poor man is like a dead man. (Nedarim 7b)

WORDS OF OUR SAGES
A person without any money is considered a fool and lacking intelligence.
(R' Shem Tov of Falaquera)

געלט איז קײַלעכדיק, אַמאָל איז עס דאָ, אַמאָל איז עס דאָרט.

Gelt iz keilechdik; amol iz es do, amol iz es dort.

[Coin] money rolls around; sometimes it's here, sometimes it's there.

MEANING

Money does not remain with its owner, but passes from hand to hand. One must treat it accordingly.

IN THE SOURCES
It is called property (נכסים) because it hides itself (נכסין) from one and reveals itself to another. And why are they called zuzim (זוזים)? – Because they move (זזים) from one to another.
[Other names:]
ממון – what you count (מונה) is valueless;
מעות – they last a short time (מעת לעת).
(Tanchuma Mattos 6)

It's cyclical: Today's rich person is not tomorrow's; the same with the poor.
(Shemos Rabbah 31:2)

IN THE SOURCES
(The saying is a parody of the Mishnah:)
The world stands on three things: on Torah, service [of God], and kind deeds.
(Avos 1:2)

אויף דריַי זאַכן שטייט די וועלט: אויף געלט, אויף געלט און – אויף געלט.

Oif drei zachen shteit di velt: oif gelt, oif gelt un – oif gelt.

The world stands on three things: on money, on money and...on money.

METAPHORICAL MEANING
Sarcastically: Money is the world's foundation.

IN THE SOURCES
Let not him who puts on his armor boast himself as he who takes it off.
(Melachim I 20:11)

ניי זיך נאָך נישט אַ בײַטל.

Nei zich noch nisht a beitel.

Don't sew a purse yet. (Don't count your chickens before they are hatched.)

MEANING
Don't make yourself a purse before you have money.

METAPHORICAL MEANING
Don't act like you have succeeded before you have accomplished the task.

דער וואָס האָט די מאה (מעה) האָט די דעה.

Der vos hot di meiah hot di deiah.

He who has the money is heeded.

(He who pays the piper calls the tune.)

MEANING
One's value in the eyes of others increases in proportion to one's wealth.

WORDS OF OUR SAGES
Money [lit. "a dinar"] cuts, money harvests; money permits, money prohibits; money appoints ignorant leaders. *(R' Moshe Chagiz)*

די גאַנצע חלה גייט אַוועק אויף אַ "המוציא."

Di gantzeh challeh geit aveck oif a "Hamotzi."

The whole challah is finished over "Hamotzi."

EXPLANATION
When the loaf of challah is small, and the number of diners is large, the entire challah will be consumed as soon as it is distributed (that is, right after the blessing "Hamotzi" is made).

METAPHORICAL MEANING
A description of a business whose earnings are eaten up by its expenses, leaving its owner with no livelihood.

IN THE SOURCES
A handful cannot satisfy the lion. *(Berachos 3b)*

אַז מ'עסט אויף דעם בייגל,
וואו קומט אַהין דער לאָך?
אין קעשענע.

*Az m'est oif dem beigel,
vu kumt ahin der loch? In kesheneh.*

When you eat the bagel, where does the hole go? – into your pocket.

METAPHORICAL MEANING
A cynical remark that expresses one's reaction to having spent much money.

IN THE SOURCES
One commits no misappropriation (me'ilah) through sound, sight, or smell. (Hence one is not liable for the enjoyment gained by merely looking at consecrated objects.)
(Pesachim 26a)

פאַרן אָנקוקן
צאָלט מען קיין געלט נישט!

Farn onkuken tzolt men kein gelt nisht!

Looking costs nothing!
(Look before you buy!)

MEANING
Advice to scrutinize the merits of a transaction before making it. Also used by a vendor to encourage customers to look at his merchandise.

INSTRUCTION
When you are about to buy or sell, first see what it is all about. Looking costs nothing; it might prevent loss and heartache, and perhaps even bring you a nice profit!

צוזאָגן און ליב האָבן קאָסט קיין געלט נישט.

Tzuzogen un lieb hoben kost kein gelt nisht.

A promise and love cost nothing.
(Talk is cheap.)

MEANING

A warning to beware of a glib talker's promises and trustworthiness. Any scoundrel is bound to promise and not fulfill, causing him to appear to love when he really hates, at no great cost to himself.

IN THE SOURCES
The simpleton believes everything. (Mishlei 14:15)

האַנדלשאַפט איז נישט קיין ברודערשאַפט.

Handelshaft iz nisht kein brudershaft.

Business connections are not family connections.

EXPLANATION

Business ties are based on considerations of whether they are worthwhile – give and take. Family ties are built on love, brotherhood, peace, and friendship.

INSTRUCTION

When relatives form business ties, it is important to distinguish between and act in an appropriate manner regarding the two relationships.

אַ געשענקט פערד קוקט מען נישט אין די ציינער.

A geshenkt ferd kukt men nisht in di tzeiner.

Don't look a gift horse in the mouth.

EXPLANATION
One who is about to purchase a horse looks at its teeth to determine its age.

METAPHORICAL MEANING
Don't criticize a gift.

IN THE SOURCES
I remember when a sela bought four se'ah, yet people in Tiberias were starving (nobody could afford to buy). (Ta'anis 19b)

אַן אָקס פאַר אַ גראָשען, אָבער דער גראָשן איז נישטאָ.

An oks far a groshen, ober der groshen iz nishto.

An ox for a penny, but who has a penny.

METAPHORICAL MEANING
A description of poverty not due to high prices.

אַז עס גייט,
גייט עס מיט אַלעמען.

Az es geit, geit es mit allemen.

When things go well, they go well all over.

MEANING
When one's luck shines, he is blessed in all he does.

IN THE SOURCES
Solicit a person with whom it goes well. (Pesachim 112a)

נעבן אַ שווערן וואָגן
איז לײַכט צו פוס גיין.

*Neben a shveren voggen
iz leicht tzu fus gein.*

It's easy to walk next to a loaded wagon.

MEANING
One who walks next to a wagon that is loaded with good things can benefit from its load and lacks nothing.

METAPHORICAL MEANING
Being next to a source of plenitude is worthwhile, for some of its abundance may spill onto you.

IN THE SOURCES
Draw near and touch one who has been anointed, and you will become anointed too. (Shevuos 47b)

Cling to a prince, and people will bow to you as well. (Sifri, Devarim 6)

WORDS OF OUR SAGES
Being friendly with the benevolent is a boon.
(Rashbag)

By the Sweat of Your Brow

נעבען אַ פעטן טאָפּ איז גוט זיך צו רייַבן.

Neben a fetten top iz gut zich tzu reiben.

It's good to rub against a fat pot.

MEANING
See previous saying.

אַז מ'שמירט פאָרט מען.

Az m'shmiert, fort men.

When you grease the wheels, the wagon goes.

(When you grease his palm, you'll get to ride.)

METAPHORICAL MEANING
A monetary gift can speed things up.

IN THE SOURCES
A man's gift broadens his space. *(Mishlei 18:16)*

קַיִן (קייען) איז נישט הבל.

Cain (kaien) iz nisht hevel.

Chewing is not worthless.

EXPLANATION

Cain (קין) was Abel's brother, a son of Adam and Eve. "Kaien" (קייַען), in Yiddish, means chewing. The saying – using the similar spellings and sounds of both words (and the fact that "Hevel" [Abel] means vain, or worthless) – implies that it is important to chew what you eat.

METAPHORICAL MEANING

One must not make light of man's physical needs.

IN THE SOURCES

"And Hashem paid notice to Abel and his offering, but not to Cain and his offering." *(Bereshis 4:4-5)*

One who has bread in his basket cannot be compared to one who has no bread in his basket. *(Yoma 18a)*

אַז מ'קוקט נישט צו מיט די אויגן, דערלייגט מען מיט דער קעשענע.

Az m'kukt nisht tzu mit di oigen, derleigt men mit der kesheneh.

If you don't look with your eyes, you'll lose from your pocket.

MEANING

If you don't pay close attention to your business dealings and property, it will cost you dearly.

IN THE SOURCES

If someone wants to lose all the money his father had left him, let him hire workers and leave them unsupervised.
(Bava Metzi'a 29b)

IN THE SOURCES

He who harasses a poor person – and knows that he is unable to repay his debt – transgresses a negative commandment.

(Rambam, Laws of Creditors and Debtors, 1:2)

"אין לי" איז די בעסטע טענה.

"Ein li" iz di besteh taineh.

"I don't have" is the best excuse.

MEANING

You can't protest against someone who claims "I don't have": "I don't have the qualifications," "I don't have the means," etc.

אַז מ'מאָנט ירושה-געלט,
צאָלט מען קבורה-געלט.

*Az m'mont yerusha-gelt,
tzolt men kvura-gelt.*

If you demand the inheritance money, you have to pay the funeral expenses.

METAPHORICAL MEANING

A person who comes to claim his rights is often asked to discharge his obligations as well. As a rule, rights and obligations go together.

אַ חוב פֿון אַ רובל אויף צען ערטער איז אַ שווערער חוב.

A choiv fun a rubel oif tzen erter iz a shverer choiv.

A debt of a ruble divided among ten creditors is a heavy debt.

MEANING

When assessing his debts, the debtor must also treat seriously the small amounts that he had borrowed from many sources, though they may seem insignificant.

גערעכנט איז האַלב באַצאָלט.

Gerechent iz halb batzolt.

Figured out is like half paid for.

MEANING

An expression of: a) satisfaction at having performed a calculation, or b) encouragement to do it. Knowing the exact amount of one's debt enables one to plan the necessary steps to repay it. It also provides extra assurance to one's creditor that the debtor knows and tends to pay back what he owes.

METAPHORICAL MEANING

A statement of contentment over the clarification of misunderstandings.

דער חשבון איז צדק,
און די קעשענע איז געשעדיקט.

*Der cheshbon iz tzedek,
un di kesheneh iz geshedikt.*

The account is correct, but the pocket is empty.

MEANING

An assertion of the fact that money vanishes quickly even when spent on the barest necessities.

פון אַ ביסל און אַ ביסל
ווערט אַ פולע שיסל.

Fun a bissel un a bissel vert a fulleh shissel.

Drop by drop the bowl fills up.

METAPHORICAL MEANING

One must not scoff at small amounts; every little bit may serve as the beginning of a great accumulation.

IN THE SOURCES

The hin (measure of volume) fills up drop by drop. (Bemidbar Rabbah 17)

Regarding charity: The pennies add up to a large sum. (Bava Basra 9b)

אז מ'שפארט נישט דעם גראשן, קומט מען נישט צום רענדל.

*Az m'shport nisht dem groshen,
kumt men nisht tzum rendel.*

If you don't save the penny, you won't have the dollar.

MEANING
Small savings add up to big ones.

IN THE SOURCES
The pennies add up to a large sum. (Bava Basra 9b)

אויפנאשן קען מען א גאנצן מאיאנטעק.

Oifnashen ken men a gantzen maiantek.

Gluttony can consume a storehouse.

METAPHORICAL MEANING
Hedonism and wastefulness can use up even the greatest wealth. It is therefore prudent to be thrifty and to act with self control.

IN THE SOURCES
"Before the silver cord is snapped asunder, and the golden bowl is shattered..." (Koheles 12:6) – Rabbi Chiya bar Nechemiah said: This refers to the throat that consumes the gold and empties out the silver. (Vayikra Rabbah 18:1)

IN THE SOURCES
Don't put all your money into one corner.
(Bereshis Rabbah 76)

בעסער צען שלעסער ווי איין דלות.

Besser tzen shlesser vi ein dalus.

Ten locks are better than one poverty.

EXPLANATION
This contains a play on words: "Dalus" (poverty) is pronounced similarly to the Hebrew "deles" (door), which gives the connection to "locks."

INSTRUCTION
It is better to hide your money in ten hiding places than to lose it all at once.

IN THE SOURCES
Better one bound bird than a hundred flying ones.
(Koheles Rabbah 4:9)

WORDS OF OUR SAGES
Reducing expenditures creates great savings, and your money is at home.
(Sefer Ha-Chinuch)

אַן אָפּגעשפּאָרטע זלאָטע איז בעסער ווי אַ פאַרדינטער רובל.

An opgeshporteh zloty iz besser vi a fardinter rubel.

A penny saved is better than a dollar earned.

METAPHORICAL MEANING
It is better to save what you have than to rely on even great amounts of income that might come your way.

By the Sweat of Your Brow

עס איז בעסער "קראַנק געוועזן" ווי "רייך געוועזן."

Es iz besser "krank gevezen" vi "reich gevesen."

Better "I was sick" than "I was rich."

EXPLANATION

You *were* sick – this means you are healthy *now*.
You *were* rich – this means you are poor *now*.

אַז מ'איז פויל, האָט מען נישט אין מויל.

Az m'iz foil, hot men nisht in moil.

The lazy person has no food.

MEANING

The lazy person who does not do his job will suffer from the deprivation he has brought on himself, as explained in the sources that follow.

IN THE SOURCES

By slothfulness the rafters sink in; and through idleness of the hands the house leaks. *(Koheles 10:18)*

"The sluggard buries his hand in the dish." – He will not bring it back to his mouth because he will not find anything to eat. *(Metzudas David, Mishlei 19:24)*

The soul of the sluggard desires, but has nothing. *(Mishlei 13:4)*

IN THE SOURCES

Great is work, for it brings honor to one who engages in it. (Nedarim 49a)

Flay carcasses in the marketplace and earn wages, and don't say, "I am a Kohen and a great man, and it's beneath my dignity." (Pesachim 113a)

WORDS OF OUR SAGES

מלאכה – מלוכה: *Work is sovereignty.*
(R' Simcha of Vitry)

IN THE SOURCES

He who buys choice meat on credit will hide from the butcher in the attic, lest the latter come and say to him: "I won't leave until you pay me."
(Rabbenu Chananel to Pesachim 114a)

Eat an onion and dwell in the shade (the protection of your house), rather than eat geese and poultry, lest your heart cultivate a greedy appetite. (Pesachim 114a)

אַרבעט איז נישט קיין שאַנד.

Arbet iz nisht kein shand.

Work is no shame.

MEANING

Praise for one who benefits from his own toil. Alternatively, disapproval of one who is worried that his work degrades him.

באָרגן מאַכט זאָרגן.

Borgen macht zorgen.

Borrowing brings worries.

MEANING

A warning about the temptation to buy on credit.

בָּארְגן און נישט אָפּגעבן מאַכט אַ בייז לעבן.

Borgen un nisht opgeben macht a beiz leben.

Borrowing and not repaying ruins one's life.

MEANING
Debtors deserve the many admonitions heaped on them, as follows in IN THE SOURCES section.

IN THE SOURCES

"Wicked is he who borrows and does not repay."
(Tehillim 33:21)

The borrower is servant to the lender. (Mishlei 22:7)

WORDS OF OUR SAGES

A loan is a worry at night and an embarrassment during the day.
(R' Yehudah Alcharizi)

A loan begins in love and ends in fighting and enmity. (R' Yehudah Alcharizi)

וואָס ביליג איז טײַער, און וואָס טײַער איז ביליג.

Vos billig iz teier, un vos teier iz billig.

Cheap is expensive, and expensive is cheap.
(Penny wise and pound foolish.)

MEANING
A warning against making business transactions based on monetary cost alone: Sometimes what was inexpensive is not worth even the little that was paid for it, so it turns out to have been expensive. On the other hand, an expensive article may prove to be worth even more than was paid for it, so that its price was low compared to its value.

IN THE SOURCES

A doctor who charges nothing is worth nothing.
(Bava Kamma 85a)

Perceiving God through Human Eyes

PERCEIVING GOD THROUGH HUMAN EYES

THE CREATOR'S EMINENCE — FAITH IN HIM AND IN DIVINE PROVIDENCE

רבונו של עולם, וואו ביסטו דאָ? וואו ביסטו נישטאָ?!

Ribono shel olam, vu bistu doh?
Vu bistu nishtoh?!

Master of the universe, where are You? Where are You not?!

MEANING
This is a believer's question accompanied by his own answer.

IN TALES OF THE CHASIDIM
Rabbi Avraham Yaakov of Sadigora was five years old when Rabbi Refael of Bershad said to him: "Here, take this silver coin. Now tell me where the Creator, blessed is He, resides."

"I'll give you two coins if you can tell me where He is not," responded the child.

(Da'as Zekenim, Ch. 12)

IN THE SOURCES
His ministering angels ask one other, "Where is the place of His glory?" in order to venerate Him. Those facing them give praise and say, "Blessed is God's glory from His place." (Kedushah)

WORDS OF OUR SAGES
O God, where can I find You? – Your place is exalted and hidden. And where will I not find You? – Your glory fills the world.
(R' Yehudah Ha-Levi)

IN THE SOURCES

Let integrity and uprightness protect me, because I have hoped for you. (Tehillim 25:21)

God is good to them that wait for Him, to the soul that seeks Him. (Eichah 3:25)

Hope to God, be strong and He will give you courage; and hope to God. (Tehillim 27:14)

אַ מענטש לעבט מיט האָפענונג;
אַלץ איז פון גאָט,
און גאָט פארלאָזט נישט.

*A mentsh lebt mit hoffenung;
altz iz fun Gott,
un Gott farlozt nisht.*

We live in hope, for all is from God, and He will not forsake us.

MEANING
See IN THE SOURCES section.

IN THE SOURCES

He Who gives life gives sustenance. (Based on Ta'anis 8b)

A boy comes into the world, loaf in hand. (Niddah 31b)

ווער עס גיט לעבן,
וועט געבן צום לעבן.

Ver es git leben, vet geben tzum leben.

He who gives life, will provide life's needs.

MEANING
An expression of trust in God, Who feeds, nourishes, and supports every living being, from the greatest to the smallest.

וואָס באַשערט דאָס ווערט.

Vos bashert dos vert.

What's decreed by Heaven will happen.
(What will be will be.)

MEANING
You can't fight God's will.

IN TALES OF THE CHASIDIM
R' Elimelech of Lizhensk and R' Zysia of Anipoli went into exile. During their travels they came to an inn where merrymaking gentiles had become quite inebriated. The drunks came over to the two Jewish brothers, who were lying down to sleep next to the furnace, beat up R' Zysia, and tossed him back to his place.

R' Elimelech became very upset and changed places with his brother, in case the hoodlums returned. The drunks came back shortly to harass the brothers again. They were about to grab R' Elimelech, when one of them said, "Let's hit the other one this time." They released R' Elimelech and grabbed R' Zysia again.

When R' Zysia returned to his place, he turned to his brother and said: "You see, what Heaven decrees happens; whoever is supposed to be beaten up will be, wherever and however."

IN THE SOURCES
If it is supposed to come upon you, it won't go away from you. (Mo'ed Katan 18b)

No one touches what is designated for another. (Yoma 38b)

WORDS OF OUR SAGES
Be calm and confident, for fear will not push away what has been decreed.
(R' Yehudah Aryeh of Modena)

IN THE SOURCES

Give Him of His own, for you and yours are His. (Avos 3:7)

Tithe in order to become rich. (Shabbos 119a)

"Who anticipated me that I should compensate him?" (Iyov 41:3) – Who performed circumcision before I gave him a son? Who built a parapet before I gave him a roof? (Vayikra Rabbah 27:2)

"'Bring the whole tithe...and try Me with this,' says God, 'and I will pour you out a blessing, that there shall be more than enough.'" (Malachi 3:10)

צום רבונו של עולם
האָט נאָך קיינער נישט צוגעלייגט.

*Tzum Ribono shel Olam
hot noch keiner nisht tzugeleigt.*

No one has ever added anything to God.

MEANING
Doing God's will yields only good and blessing, never a loss.

IN THE SOURCES

Man must praise God for every single breath he breathes. (Yalkut Tehillim 889)

For it is the duty of all creatures to give thanks to You, Hashem our God...and to praise... (From the Morning Prayer for Sabbaths and Festivals)

צו דאַנקען און צו לויבן
דעם וואָס זיצט אויבן.

*Tzu danken un tzu loiben
dem vos zitzt oiben.*

Give thanks and praise to Him Who dwells above.

MEANING
An expression of praise to God.

How Man Perceives God

אַ מענטש נעמט זיך
גאָרנישט אַליין.

A mentsh nemt zich gornisht alein.

No one takes anything unto himself by himself.

MEANING
Everything comes to a person from Heaven; he has no power to add to it or subtract from it.

IN THE SOURCES
No one can infringe on what has been decreed for his fellow...even to a hair's-breadth. (Yoma 38b)

Even he who is in charge of water holes has been appointed by Heaven. (Berachos 58a)

אַ מענטש טוט נישט
גאָרנישט אַליין.

A mentsh tut nisht gornisht alein.

Man does nothing for himself by himself.

MEANING
Man cannot do things of his own power, without it having been decreed, and is not master over his future and destiny.

IN THE SOURCES
Man does not lift a finger below unless it has been decreed above. (Chullin 7b)

WORDS OF OUR SAGES
Without God, it is impossible to cross the threshold of one's house; with God, it is possible to split the sea.
(R' Mordechai of Lechovitz)

אַ מענטש טראַכט און דער אויבערשטער מאַכט.

A mentsh tracht un der Oibershter macht.

Man proposes and God disposes.

אַ מענטש טראַכט און דער אויבערשטער לאַכט.

A mentsh tracht un der Oibershter lacht.

Man plans and God laughs.

MEANING

Man thinks he is capable of planning his steps, but they really depend on God; He can nullify or make a mockery of them if they are against His will.

IN THE SOURCES

There are many thoughts in a man's heart; but the counsel of God shall prevail. (Mishlei 19:21)

...and nations mutter in vain...He Who sits in heaven laughs. (Tehillim 2:1, 4)

אַ געפֿאַלענעם העלפֿט גאָט.

A gefallenem helft Gott.

God upholds all who fall.
(Tehillim 145:14)

MEANING

"Gefallenem" has two meanings in Yiddish: one who thinks little of himself, or one who has fallen down. The saying applies to those who have fallen in spirit and see themselves as inferior: God supports and raises them. It is also used to comfort one who has literally fallen down.

IN THE SOURCES

I dwell on high, in holiness; yet with the contrite and lowly in spirit – reviving the spirits of the lowly, reviving the hearts of the contrite. (Yeshayahu 57:15)

WORDS OF OUR SAGES

When a Jew falls, he falls into God's lap.
(R' Mordechai Yosef of Izbica)

בײַ דעם אױבערשטן דארף מען אַ אײביקער בעטלער זײַן.

Bei der Oibershten darf men a eibicker betler zein.

Before God one must always be a beggar.

EXPLANATION
"Betler" in Yiddish means a beggar (for money), as well as a supplicant (for a favor). The saying sounds like it refers to the first meaning, but when more deeply considered, it refers to the second meaning.

IN TALES OF THE CHASIDIM
R' Sar Shalom of Belz was sitting at his table surrounded by many of his Chasidim, who were absorbing living Torah from his actions. Suddenly, a woman burst into the room, and in a heartrending cry begged the Rebbe to pray that she bear a viable child. The Rebbe gave her his blessing, and she left in a much better mood.

After her departure, the Rebbe said to his Chasidim, "Did you see that? The woman has been blessed by me many times, with no results as yet. In spite of that, she keeps coming back again and again... Contemplate it and learn from her: If she does not despair of returning and entreating me – mere flesh and blood who has already blessed her many times – how much more so should we continue to entreat the King of Kings always and in every situation!"

It has been said that because the woman so inspired those present, she was rewarded with a son! *(Admorei Belz, I:320)*

IN THE SOURCES
Whoever does not have [a treasury of reward], I shall make [one] for him and pay him from it, as it is written (Shemos 33:19): "I will show favor to whomever I choose to favor."
(Midrash Rabbah, Ki Sissa 45)

WORDS OF OUR SAGES
The greatest treasure is the treasure of an unearned gift. The only people who can receive such a gift are those who know that it comes not from their own deeds, but from God's grace.
(Sifsey Kohen to Va'eschanan)

One must pray as a poor man begging for his needs, because "The poor man speaks entreatingly" (Mishlei 18:23) – and not as one who asks for something he does not need, who requests neither with a contrite heart nor a broken spirit.
(Rabbenu Yonah to Avos 2)

דער אויבערשטער גיט די קעלט נאָך די קליידער.

Der Oibershter git di kelt noch di kleider.

The Almighty tailors the cold after our clothing.

METAPHORICAL MEANING

Hardships are imposed on man according to his ability to bear them.

IN THE SOURCES

He provides snow like wool, scatters frost like ashes; He flings His ice like crumbs... (Tehillim 147:16, 17)
"Snow like wool" – The amount of snow will be proportional to the woolen garments man possesses.
"Frost like ashes" – Corresponding to the amount of firewood needed to provide relief from the frost.
"His ice like crumbs" – According to the amount of bread available to alleviate hunger on freezing days. (Ibid., in the commentaries)

According to the camel is its load. (Kesubos 67a)

אַז גאָט גיט, גיבן גוטע לייט אויך.

Az Gott git, gibben guteh leit oich.

When God gives, so will all good-hearted people give.

MEANING

Only when God wishes to bestow of His goodness upon one of His creatures, will the hearts of the generous become aroused to give him something.

IN THE SOURCES

Put not your trust in noble men, in man who is incapable of deliverance.... Fortunate is he whom the God of Jacob helps, whose expectation is on Hashem, his God. (Tehillim 146:3, 5)

And find grace and good favor in the eyes of God and man. (Mishlei 3:4)

How Man Perceives God

אַנטקעגן דעם אויבערשטן
קען מען קיין חכם נישט זײַן.

*Antkeggen dem Oibershten
ken men kein chochem nisht zein.*

No one can outsmart the Almighty.

METAPHORICAL MEANING
It doesn't pay to try to circumvent God's will.

IN TALES OF THE CHASIDIM
R' Menachem Mendel of Kotzk asked R' Menachem Mendel of Warka: "What new insight did King Solomon, the wisest of men, provide for us?" In response to the latter's silence, the former continued: "He taught us that, 'Neither wisdom nor understanding nor counsel avails against God,' " from which we learn that it doesn't pay to be too clever.

IN THE SOURCES
Neither wisdom nor understanding nor counsel avails against God.
(Mishlei 21:30)

דער אויבערשטער שטראָפט נישט
מיט ביידע הענט.

Der Oibershter shtraft nisht mit beideh hent.

The Almighty punishes not with both hands.

METAPHORICAL MEANING
God's kindness is evident, even in times of distress.

IN THE SOURCES
I have wounded and I will heal. (Devarim 32:39)

God is merciful even in His anger. (Tanchuma Vayera 9)

MAMMA USED TO SAY

IN THE SOURCES

Even the person for whom a miracle is performed is unaware of the miracle. (Niddah 31a)

How a man doesn't feel that God helps him! (Yoma 22b)

מ'וויסט נישט
פֿאַר וואָס גאָט צו דאַנקען.

M'veist nisht far vos Gott tzu danken.

No one knows what to thank God for.

IN TALES OF THE CHASIDIM

The Seer of Lublin told the following story:

An anti-Semitic official had a particular penchant for harassing a certain God-fearing Jew who lived in his town. The Jew was in the habit of getting up before dawn and going to the synagogue to study before praying. The official decided to send his servants to dig a deep ditch across the Jew's route, so that the one he abhorred would fall into it during his next walk in the dark to the synagogue.

What did the Holy One, blessed is He, do? He arranged for an important guest to call on His faithful servant, with whom he proceeded to learn Torah deep into the night. The next morning, the Jew left the house a little later than usual, and by the dawn's light he was able to see and avoid the ditch.

The official arrived at the site and noticed that his plot was unsuccessful. He hurried to the synagogue to ask the Jew why he was late that day. Upon hearing about the unexpected guest who had saved his host, the official arose and cried out: "How great is the God of the Jews Who protects the feet of His pious ones from all evil!"

In view of the above, the Seer explained the following verse: "Praise God, all nations; extol Him all peoples. For His kindness has overwhelmed us..." *(Tehillim 117:1, 2).* Now, because

His kindness has overwhelmed us, why should all nations praise Him?!

The answer is that sometimes we don't praise God for miracles, because we are not aware of them; only the nations, who know of their own scheming against us, realize that God saves us from their hands.

איידער אָנצוקומען צום בעסטן מענטשן, בעסער אָנצוקומען צו "אין כאלוקינו".

Eider ontzukummen tzum besten mentshen, besser ontzukummen tzu "Ein Kelokeinu."

Rather than depend on [or: come to] the best of people, it is better to depend on [or: come to] "Ein Kelokenu" [None is like our God.]

EXPLANATION
"Ontzukummen" means to depend on, as well as to arrive at a destination. The saying incorporates both meanings:
1) Instead of depending on kindnesses of the generous, it is better to rely on our God, for "Ein Kelokenu" – "There is none like our God."
2) Entreat and implore Him from the beginning of the prayers until we reach "Ein Kelokenu" which appears at the end of the service.

IN THE SOURCES
"And in [the dove's] mouth there was a plucked-off olive leaf." – She said: Better that my food be bitter, like the olive, from the hand of God, than sweet like honey, from the hand of man.
(Rashi to Bereshis 8:11)

It is better to take refuge in God than to trust in man. It is better to take refuge in God than to trust in noble men. (Tehillim 118:8, 9)

Don't put your trust in noble men.... Fortunate is he whom the God of Jacob helps, whose reliance is on Hashem, his God.
(Tehillim 146:3, 5)

WORDS OF OUR SAGES

If we believe in the Creator's loving-kindness, there are no questions; if we don't believe, there are no answers.
(R' Yaakov Aryeh of Radzymin)

"His greatness is unfathomable."
(Tehillim 145:3) – *One may grasp God's greatness through faith, not by investigation.*
(R' Moshe of Kobrin)

אויף גאָט טאָר מען
קיין קשיא נישט פֿרעגן.

Oif Gott tor men kein kashyeh nisht freggen.

One must not question God's actions.

MEANING
A Jew is aware of the fact that all of God's actions are truth and good, and that any question he has concerning them stems from his own inadequacy and God's inscrutability.

IN TALES OF THE CHASIDIM
Following the death of the daughter of R' Menachem Mendel of Zdunska-Wola, her father could find no consolation for his sorrow. He acceded to his family's pleas that he visit R' Menachem Mendel of Kotzk.

When he came in to see the Rebbe, the latter presented him with a difficulty concerning a certain gemara. The rabbi of Zdunska-Wola immediately resolved the difficulty. The Rebbe then raised a problem regarding a particular tosefos, with the same results.

After additional exchanges of the same nature, the Rebbe of Kotzk said: "If there is no room for questioning the gemara, the gemara must be right. The same can be said for the tosefos. If so, there is clearly no justification for questioning God, for He is undoubtedly right."

How Man Perceives God

ווען גאָט דערפרייט איז קיין מאָל נישט צו שפּעט.

Ven Gott derfreit iz kein mol nisht tzu shpet.

When God rejoices, it is never too late [for us, too].

MEANING

A celebration that comes from the Source of joy is a true and complete one; it can never be celebrated too late.

וואָס גאָט וועט געבן דאָס וועט זיַין.

Vos Gott vet gebben dos vet zein.

What God gives endures.

MEANING

Only God's gifts are authentic, hence they are durable.

IN THE SOURCES

Gifts that do not come from God will not endure. Korach the Jew, and Haman the gentile were destroyed because their gifts did not come from God; rather, they seized them unto themselves.
(Bemidbar Rabbah 22:6)

איין גאָט אויף אַלע שׂונאים

Ein Gott oif alleh son'im

One God against all enemies

MEANING

A statement that illustrates God's might, directed at someone whose faith and trust need strengthening.

IN THE SOURCES

God is with me, to help me, and I will see [the defeat of] my enemies. (Tehillim 118:7)

The Virtuous and Their Ways

THE VIRTUOUS AND THEIR WAYS

A. ADVICE AND GUIDANCE FOR SERVING THE CREATOR

פֿון אַ קינד קען מען זיך לערנען דרײַ זאַכן: גייט נישט אַרום ליידיק, שטענדיק צופֿרידן, ווען ס'פֿעלט אים עפּעס שרײַט ער "טאַטע."

Fun a kind ken men zich lernen drei zachen: geit nisht arum leidik; shtendik tzufrieden; ven s'felt im eppes shreit er "Tatteh."

We may learn three things from a baby: he is never idle; he is always happy; when he needs something, he cries, "Daddy."
(R' Moshe Leib of Sassov)

INSTRUCTION

Take note! The three things we can learn from a baby are lessons in serving God.

IN THE SOURCES

God said to the Jews: Be conscientious in prayer, for there is no better virtue...even if a person is not worthy of having his prayers answered and of receiving beneficence, if he prays and entreats exceedingly, I will bestow My kindness upon him.
(Tanchuma Vayera 1)

The Rashal in his Responsa (98) affirmed that the Rash said that after studying Kabbalah he prays like a day-old baby.
(Mishnah Berurah 98:1)

IN THE SOURCES
He who walks in innocence will walk securely.
(Mishlei 10:9)

He will guard the steps of His devout ones.
(Shemuel I, 2:9)

WORDS OF OUR SAGES
A person is where his thoughts are.
(R' Yisrael Ba'al Shem Tov)

WORDS OF CHASIDIM
It is better to eat in preparation for prayer, than to pray in preparation for eating.

אַז מ'גייט גלייך, פאַלט מען נישט.

Az m'geit gleich, falt men nisht.

If you walk straight, you will not fall.

METAPHORICAL MEANING
He who lives honestly will not stumble.

ס'איז בעסער צו שטיין ביַים טאָפּ און אין זינען האָבן דעם סידור, איידער צו שטיין ביַי דעם סידור און אין זינען האבן דעם טאָפּ.

S'iz besser tzu shtein beim top un in zinnen hobben dem Siddur, eider tzu shtein bei dem Siddur un in zinnen hobben dem top.

It is better to stand by the pot on the stove and think about the Siddur [prayers], than to stand [in prayer] by the Siddur and think about the pot on the stove.

METAPHORICAL MEANING
A person's thoughts say more than his actions about his spiritual state.

The Virtuous and Their Ways

פֿון זיך נישט אַרויסקוקן,
צו יענעם נישט אַרײַנקוקן,
און זיך נישט צו מיינען.

Fun zich nisht aroiskuken, tzu yenem nisht areinkuken, un zich nisht tzu meinen.

Don't look away from yourself; don't scrutinize another; and don't intend it for yourself!

(R' Menachem Mendel of Kotzk)

INSTRUCTION
These are three pointers for self-improvement:
1) Always observe what is going on inside you,
2) don't be critical of another person's faults, and
3) do this for the sake of Heaven, not for selfish reasons.

אז מ'איז אפּגעדאַוונט
איז מען באַפֿרייט.

Az m'iz opgedavent iz men bafreit.

When you finish praying, you are free.

MEANING
A Jew knows that, due to its importance, prayer takes priority over any other occupation; only after he has prayed may he engage in other business.

IN THE SOURCES
One must refrain from becoming involved in his own needs, or setting out on a trip, until he has prayed...neither eat nor drink...even learning is forbidden.
(Shulchan Aruch 89)

WORDS OF OUR SAGES

King David asked God that he merit having people read this holy book while focusing on the words' inner meaning and investigating their secrets ...and that their hearts melt like water. Then will awaken in them a strong desire to cling to God and to serve Him wholeheartedly.

(Introduction to Mikdash Me'at to Tehillim)

טיי מיט תהלים קענען נישט שאדן, נאָר זיי דאַרפן זיין וואַרים.

Tei mit Tehillim kennen nisht shaden, nor zei darfen zein varim.

Tea and Tehillim can never hurt – but [to help] they must be warm.

EXPLANATION
Among East European Jews, "Tehillim zoggers" [Psalms sayers] were common. They often sat in the house of study, warming themselves by the furnace, reciting Psalms and drinking tea.

MEANING
The saying uses the accepted notion that tea tastes better and is more beneficial when hot, to emphasize the importance of reciting Tehillim "warmly," that is, with feeling.

IN THE SOURCES

He opens the gate to those who knock in repentance; all believe that He has an open hand.
(From the Musaf prayer service of Rosh Hashanah and Yom Kippur)

He knocked on the Gates of Mercy and they opened for him. (Megillah 12b)

WORDS OF OUR SAGES

He who knocks persistently succeeds. (R' Moshe ben Ezra)

אַז מ'קלאַפט אָן – עפנט מען.

Az m'klapt on, effent men.

If you knock on the door, it will be opened.

MEANING
If we knock on the Gates of Heaven with repentance, prayer, and charity, we will be answered.

אַלטע זאַכן פֿאַרריכטן,
אוּן נײַע נישט קאַליע מאַכן.

Alteh zachen farrichten,
un neieh nisht kalyeh machen.

Repair the old,
and don't ruin the new.

METAPHORICAL INSTRUCTION
Guidance for serving God: Purify the old, which you have sullied, and guard from contamination through sin that which is pure.

IN TALES OF THE CHASIDIM
During the engagement party between the children of R' Yisrael of Ruzhin and R' Hirsh of Rimanov, the former took the floor and said: "It is customary at this time to share our yichus [our lineage] with each other." He began: "My great-grandfather was R' Dov Ber of Mezritch, my grandfather was his son, the malach [angel], and my father was R' Shalom Shachna. And now, Mechutan, it's your turn to tell us of your illustrious lineage!"

R' Hirsh answered: "I was orphaned at an early age, and I did not get to know my parents. I cannot therefore sing their praises, but I was told that they were very good and honest people. As a child, I was apprenticed to a tailor, and although I was very young, I followed the path of truth and was most careful to repair the old, and not ruin the new..."

"Enough, enough, Mechutan!" said the Ruzhiner. "I don't need to hear more than that!" And they got down to the business of signing the agreement.

IN THE SOURCES

(The saying is based on the following verse, the changes serving as a seeming interpretation:) "The sum of the matter, when all is said and done: Fear God and observe His commandments!"
(Koheles 12:13)

"סוף דבר הכל נשמע" — לערנען תורה, דינען דעם בורא, און פון קיינעם נישט האבן מורא.

"Sof davar hakol nishma" — lernen Toireh, dienen dem Boireh, un fun keinem nisht hobben moireh.

"The sum of the matter, when all is said and done," is: Learn Torah, serve the Creator, and fear no one.

MEANING

A statement that serves as a typical synopsis of a conversation between Jews.

IN THE SOURCES

He who took trouble [to prepare] on the eve of the Sabbath will eat on the Sabbath. (Avodah Zarah 3a)

WORDS OF OUR SAGES

How does one serve God? Among chasidim I have heard it said that as you make your bed, so will you sleep in it; as you sleep, so will you get up; as you get up, so will you be awake; and as you are awake, so will you serve...
(R' Zusya of Hanipoli)

ווי מ'בעט זיך אויס אזוי שלאָפט מען.

Vi m'bet zich ois azoi shloft men.

As you make your bed, so will you sleep in it.

METAPHORICAL MEANING

The degree of satisfaction obtained is proportional to the effort put into preparation.

The Virtuous and Their Ways

לאָמיר נישט זאָרגן וואָס וועט זיין מאָרגן, לאָמיר בעסער פאַרריכטן דעם הײַנט און דעם נעכטן.

Lommir nisht zorgen vos vet zein morgen, lommir besser farrichten dem heint un dem nechten.
(From R' Mendele of Worka's songs)

Don't worry about tomorrow; better to fix today and yesterday.

INSTRUCTION
It is futile to worry about the future, which is unknown. Better concern oneself with what is certain – what we can improve in the present and correct from the past.

IN THE SOURCES
Don't worry about tomorrow's trouble, for you know not what the day will bring. Perhaps you will not be here when tomorrow comes, and so you have worried about a world which is not yours.
(Yevamos 63b)

WORDS OF OUR SAGES
Instead of wondering what you'll do tomorrow, it's better to repair what you did yesterday.
(R' Ze'ev Wolf of Zhitomir)

אַזוי לאַנג ווי דער אײַזן איז הייס קלאַפט מען.

Azoi lang vi der eizen iz heiss klapt men.

Strike while the iron is hot.

METAPHORICAL MEANING
As long as it is still possible to accomplish something, one must keep trying.

IN THE SOURCES
As long as a piece of iron is in the fire, one can make of it whatever vessel he wishes. So it is with the evil inclination: there is no other remedy for it but the study of Torah, which is like fire.
(Avos d'Rabbi Nasan 16:3)

IN THE SOURCES

There are three gifts in the world. He who has earned one of them has received what the world most desires: if he has wisdom, he has everything; similarly, power or wealth. When is this true? – When they are gifts from Heaven and come by virtue of Torah.
(Bemidbar Rabbah 22:6)

Behold, I have given you a wise and understanding heart, such that there has never been anyone like you...also wealth and honor, as there has never been among the kings like you...
(Melachim I, 3:12, 13)

WORDS OF OUR SAGES

One's gifts are like items entrusted for safekeeping.
(R' Avraham Chasdai)

שׂכל איז אַ געשאַנק, געלט איז אַ געשאַנק. וואויל איז דעם וואָם דינט מיט די געשאַנקען דעם אויבערשטן וואָם האָט אים געשענקט.

Sechel iz a geshank, gelt iz a geshank. Voil iz dem vos dient mit di geshanken dem Oibershten vos hot im geshenkt.

The intellect is a gift, and wealth is a gift. Happy is he who serves with his gifts the Almighty Who has given them.

MEANING
See IN THE SOURCES section.

דאָרט וואו ס'איז ענג דאָרטן רײַסט זיך.

Dort vu s'iz eng dorten reisst zich.

It rips where it's tight.

METAPHORICAL MEANING
Problems surface at vulnerable points. (Get yourself in a tight spot, and you'll get hurt!)

אַז מ'קען נישט אַריבער גייט מען אַרונטער.

Az m'ken nisht aribber geit men arunter.

When you can't go over, go underneath.

METAPHORICAL MEANING
When you can't do what you wish, you have to settle for what's available. When you can't win, you have to know how to lose!

אַז מ'קען נישט אַריבער מוז מען אַריבער!

Az m'ken nisht aribber muz men aribber!

When you can't go over, you have to go over!

INSTRUCTION
If something seems impossible to overcome, it's because surrender is considered to be an option. Tell yourself that there is no choice but to succeed, and you will be able to do so!

IN THE SOURCES

Whoever presses time is pressed by time; whoever forgoes pressing it will succeed. (Berachos 64a)

If you see that time is against you, don't fight it: whoever vies with time, succumbs to it; whoever gives way to it, overcomes it. (Yalkut Shemos 168)

If you stand against a wave, it will wash you away; if you don't, it will not. (Bereshis Rabbah 44:18)

> **WORDS OF OUR SAGES**
> *Everyone thinks that if you can't go over, you should go underneath. I maintain that if you can't go underneath, you should go over.*
> (R' Menachem Mendel of Kotzk)

אַז מ'קען נישט אַרונטער גייט מען אַריבער.

Az m'ken nisht arunter geit men aribber.

When you can't go underneath, go over.

INSTRUCTION

When you can't deal with a problem by way of compromise or concession, overcome it by disregarding ("skipping over") its difficulties and pitfalls.

> **WORDS OF OUR SAGES**
> *People say, "When you can't go under, go over." I say, "Always try to go over!"*
> (R' Yosef Yitzchak of Lubavitch, Igros Moharyatz I)

אֲפִילוּ מ'קען אַרונטער בעסער לכתחילה אַריבער!

Afilu m'ken arunter besser l'chat'chila aribber!

Even when you can go underneath, it's better to go over!

INSTRUCTION

Even when less effort will yield satisfactory results, it is better to try and get everything through maximal effort.

כבוד זוך איך נישט, אָבער דעם אומכבוד וויל איך נישט.

*Koved zuch ich nisht,
ober dem umkoved vill ich nisht.*

I'm not looking for honor, but neither do I want dishonor.

MEANING

Honor is deceptive, so there is no reason to seek it. Dishonor is humiliating and disgraceful; one must therefore distance oneself from it.

IN THE SOURCES

There is no better quality in the world than humility.
(Osiyos d'Rabbi Akiva, ק׳ 50)

Sometimes you may ignore your brother's lost object: for example, if [you are] an old man and it is inconsistent with [your] dignity.
(Rashi to Devarim 22:1)

WORDS OF OUR SAGES

Humility is the golden mean between pride and humiliation (dishonor).
(Rambam)

The lowly do not feel what they lack, and don't try to raise themselves up.
(R' Yosef of Lechovitz)

אַז עס איז נישט ווי איך וויל, וויל איך ווי עס איז.

Az es iz nisht vi ich vill, vill ich vi es iz.

If it's not as I want it, I want it as it is.

MEANING

We must accept what we cannot change.

WORDS OF OUR SAGES

If your life is not as you will it, adapt your will to your life.
(R' Mordechai of Lechovitz)

MAMMA USED TO SAY

WORDS OF OUR SAGES

Just to go through the motions? Absolutely not! All or nothing!
(R' Menachem Mendel of Kotzk)

Only horses walk in the middle of the road.
(R' Menachem Mendel of Kotzk)

IN THE SOURCES

How long will you keep hopping between two opinions? (Melachim I, 18:21)

אָדער גאָר, אָדער גאָר נישט

Oder gor, oder gor nisht

All or nothing

MEANINGS

a. An expression of surprise: All or nothing?! This is hardly the path to choose. One must rather seek out the middle way between two extremes.
b. Establishing an approach: All or nothing! When conditions do not allow for compromising or taking the middle road, one must choose the extreme.

אָדער אַהין, אָדער אַהער

Oder ahin, oder aher

Either here, or there

INSTRUCTION
Decide!

IN TALES OF THE CHASIDIM

R' Avraham of Porissov was sitting in the house of study, deep in study. The only sound to pierce the silence was that of the footsteps of a young scholar walking to and fro. Something in those steps attracted R' Avraham's attention: they sounded restless, slack, and unstable.

R' Avraham got up, approached the young man, and said: "While you were walking from here to there, you obviously thought that it was better there. I also understood when you came back here from there: you thought it was better here. But now, why are you going back there? Decide where you want to be!"

The Virtuous and Their Ways

די אויגן זאָלן נישט זען,
וואָלטן די הענט נישט גענומען.

*Di oigen zollen nisht zen,
volten di hent nisht genummen.*

If the eyes wouldn't see, the hands wouldn't take.

MEANING
If the eyes would not look at what causes craving, the heart would not desire and the hands would not take.

IN THE SOURCES
"...so that you do not follow your heart and eyes after which you stray." – The heart and eyes are the body's spies, and its procurers of sin: the eye sees, the heart desires, and the limbs commit the sin. (Rashi to Bemidbar 15:39)

The evil inclination only bears sway over what a person's eyes see. (Sotah 8a)

WORDS OF OUR SAGES
Closing the eyes is the best deterrent to desire.
(Rabbi Shlomo ben Gevirol)

א בושה איז נאר צו גנבענען –
נישט אפצוגעבן.

*A busheh iz nor zu ganvenen –
nisht optzugeben.*

Stealing is shameful; returning is not.

METAPHORICAL INSTRUCTION
It is appropriate to be ashamed when sinning, but not when making amends!

IN THE SOURCES
Like the shame of a thief when he is caught.
(Yirmeyahu 2:26)

אַ לאַנגער צדיק

A langer tzaddik

An overly righteous person

EXPLANATION

In Yiddish, the final form of the letter "tzadi[k]" is called "langer [a long] tzadi[k]." The saying thus describes a person whose righteousness is oversized.

IN THE SOURCES
Don't be overly righteous.
(Koheles 7:16)

WORDS OF OUR SAGES
Just as the evil inclination tries to incite a person to sin, it also incites him to be overly righteous.
(R' Yechiel Michel of Zloczow)

A person must always be moral and honest, but not overly righteous or excessively pious, because this is the type of conceit that is sewn with threads of sadness and boredom.
(R' Isaac of Komarna)

ניע פאַסטע, ניע גנבע!

Nie fasteh, nie ganveh!

Don't fast – and don't steal!

METAPHORICAL INSTRUCTION
Don't sin and later don the guise of ultra-piety.

IN THE SOURCES
[The Jews of Isaiah's generation asked:] "Why, when we fasted, did You not see?" [God answered through the prophet:] "Because on your fast day you see to your business" – (Rashi: You busy yourselves with obtaining your personal needs, even by thievery and lawlessness.) *– "Is such the fast I desire?!"*
(Yeshayahu 58:3, 5)

דער נאַר שטופּט.

Der nar shtupt.

The fool pushes.

MEANINGS

a. Said in reaction to a person's senseless act: The foolishness in him pushed him to do something irrational... (Fools walk in where wise men fear to tread.)
b. A rationalization of having succumbed to the evil inclination: It's very difficult to overcome when the evil inclination, called "the fool," pushes and urges on!

IN THE SOURCES
An old king and a fool [the evil inclination].
(Koheles 4:13)

A person does not commit a sin unless a spirit of foolishness enters into him.
(Sotah 3a)

WORDS OF OUR SAGES
Nothing is as clever and shrewd, cunning and seductive, as the evil inclination. Then why is it called "a fool"? – Because it does business with fools.
(R' Leibeleh Eiger)

ווײַל דו ווילסט, דווקא "נישט," מאָרגן "יאָ," הײַנט "נישט."

Veil du vilst, davka "nisht," morgen "yo," heint "nisht."

Because you want to, the answer is "no"; tomorrow "yes," today "no."

MEANING

This is a defiant negative response to someone who is strong-willed. It can be effective in man's struggle with his evil inclination.

IN THE SOURCES
"...refrain from pursuing your own needs [on the Sabbath]" (Yeshayahu 58:13) – Your desires are forbidden; those of Heaven are permitted.
(Avnei Nezer on Shabbos 113a)

WORDS OF OUR SAGES
What one has the urge to do, he should not do.
(R' Menachem Mendel Schneerson of Lubavitch)

MAMMA USED TO SAY

IN THE SOURCES
(The statement is a play on words of:) The gates of tears are never locked.
(Berachos 32b)

WORDS OF OUR SAGES
The gates of excuses are never locked – because there are no such gates. Therefore, don't argue with the evil inclination! It will always find an excuse, and you will have to fight it constantly...
(R' Menachem Mendel of Warka)

די טויערן פֿון פֿאַרענטפֿערן זענען נישט געשלאָסן געוואָרן.

Di toiern fun farentfern zennen nisht geshlossen gevoren.

The gates of excuses are never locked.

METAPHORICAL MEANING
One will always find "excuses" to justify his behavior.

WORDS OF OUR SAGES
I am not afraid of the pains of illness. What worries me is the pampering that lingers on...
(R' Menachem Mendel of Kotzk)

דאָס אויפֿשטיין איז שווערער ווי דאָס פֿאַלן.

Dos oifshtein iz shverer vi dos fallen.

Getting up is harder than the fall.

MEANING
Recovery requires more spiritual strength than does struggling with difficulties.

אַלֵיין איז די נשמה רֵיין.

Alein iz di neshomeh rein.

His soul is spotless
who acts alone.
(Don't rely on others;
do it yourself.)

MEANING
A saying in praise of one who acts alone, when working with others may cause social and spiritual complications.

אַז די נשמה וועט זײַן אויסגעהיילט וועט דער גוף ווערן אויסגעהיילט.

Az di neshomeh vet zein oisgeheilt vet der guf verren oisgeheilt.

When the soul is healed
the body will be healed.

MEANING
The sturdiness of the body is linked to that of the soul.

IN THE SOURCES

If I could only be in a travelers' inn in the desert, and leave my people, go away from them, for they are all...a band of traitors.
(Yirmeyahu 9:1)

WORDS OF OUR SAGES

Each of our 248 limbs is nourished by a particular mitzvah that relates to that limb...The vitality of each limb is dependent on its corresponding mitzvah. We must therefore be very careful with every mitzvah, for if we neglect one of them, its corresponding limb will lose all its vitality.
(Toldos Yaakov Yosef, Introduction)

אַ קלײנער לאָך אין גוף איז אַ גרױסער לאָך אין די נשמה.

*A kleiner loch in guf
iz a groisser loch in di neshomeh.*

A small hole in the body is a large hole in the soul.

MEANING

Even a slight illness in one's body can cause considerable disturbances in the soul.

IN THE SOURCES

Being healthy is one of the ways of [serving] God, because a person who is ill can't understand or know anything about the Creator. (Rambam, Hilchos De'os 4:1)

WORDS OF OUR SAGES

A person must take care of his body, because when it is ill his soul becomes weak, too. (R' Yisrael Ba'al Shem Tov)

A little hole in the body causes a big hole in the soul. (R' Dov Ber of Mezritch)

תורה איז די בעסטע סחורה.

Torah iz di besteh s'choireh.

Torah is the best merchandise.

MEANING

This is said with the intention of praising those who study Torah, or to encourage its study.

IN THE SOURCES

Regarding any kind of merchandise, the owner worries that it will depreciate in value or be stolen. It is not so with Torah.
(Pesikta Zutarta, beginning of Terumah)

Every occupation sustains a person while he is young; when he is old, he goes hungry. The Torah is different: It stands him in good stead in his youth, and it provides him with a future and hope in old age.
(Yerushalmi, end of Kiddushin, 4:12)

גיס בוימל אויף דעם לאָמפּ אַזוי לאַנג ווי עס ברענט נאָך.

Giess boimel oif dem lomp azoi lang vi es brennt noch.

Add oil to the lamp as long as the flame burns.

METAPHORICAL MEANING
Continue achieving as long as it is possible.

IN THE SOURCES
Add oil to the lamp to keep it burning; once the light snuffs out, the oil is useless. (Yalkut Shimoni, Koheles 989)

Repent while you still have the strength; add oil to the lamp while it still burns. (Ibid., 979)

Perform while you can find, and it is available to you, and you still have it. (Explanation: Perform tzedakah as long as you can find someone to give it to, have the means, and are alive – before you die.) (Shabbos 151b)

וואָס מ'נעמט זיך נישט אַליין האָט מען נישט.

Vos m'nemt zich nisht alein, hot men nisht.

If you don't acquire it yourself, you won't have it.

MEANING
An expression in praise of using personal effort to attain (spiritual) accomplishments.

IN THE SOURCES
If I am not for myself, who will be for me? (Avos 1:14)

Everything is in God's hands except the fear of God. (Berachos 33b)

WORDS OF OUR SAGES
A man can fast from Sabbath to Sabbath and remain a lustful person.
(R' Aharon of Karlin)

אַ פֿערד פֿאָרט נאָך לייפציג,
און קומט פֿון לייפציג,
און בלייבט אַ פֿערד.

A ferd fort noch Leipzig, un kumt fun Leipzig, un bleibt a ferd.

A horse travels to Leipzig, and returns from Leipzig, and remains a horse.

EXPLANATION
Leipzig served as the site for big fairs. It offered its clever visitors many opportunities to broaden their horizons in many areas of life – but not to the horses that came.

METAPHORICAL MEANING
When a Jew does things that could elevate him, but such behavior does not derive from his inner self, his essence is not changed.

IN TALES OF THE CHASIDIM
A man came before Rabbi Yisrael of Ruzhin and began to boast of his "religious" conduct:

"I refrain from eating cooked food on weekdays; I drink only cold water; I do not sleep in a bed; I put nails into my shoes to pierce my flesh; in the winter I roll in the snow to atone for my sins; and every day I receive 39 lashes."

The Rebbe detected the conceit in the man's words, took him over to the window, and pointed at a horse that was happily rolling in the snow.

"Do you see that horse?" he asked. "It drinks cold water; never tastes cooked food; sleeps on the ground; has nails in its hooves; rolls in the snow; and is whipped over forty times a day – yet he remains a horse...."

מיט זיך אַליין איז מען נאָך נישט פאַרטיג!

Mit zich alein iz men noch nisht fartig!

We have not yet completed ourselves!

MEANING
Our reaction when confronted with the need to work at perfecting others: We have yet to attain self-perfection; how then can we occupy ourselves in perfecting others?!

IN TALES OF THE CHASIDIM
Said R' Chaim of Tzanz:

The flame of God burned within me when I was young: I believed that I would return the whole world to good. As I grew older, my enthusiasm waned, and I said: "I see that I will not be able to fix the entire world, so I will try to improve the people of my own city." Years passed, and I realized that I had bitten off more than I could chew. I then decided that it would be enough to better my own family. Now that I am old, I no longer dream. My only prayer is that I should improve myself.

IN THE SOURCES
Improve yourself, before demanding it of others.
(Bava Metzia 107b)

WORDS OF OUR SAGES
"Appoint judges and officers for yourself..."
(Devarim 16:18) – *Scrutinize your actions and check yourself before you judge others.*
(R' Menachem Mendel of Kotzk)

IN THE SOURCES

Nachum of Gamzu used to respond to any difficulty that befell him, by saying: "This also [gam zu] is for the best."

Once the Jews needed to send a gift to the emperor. They said, "Let us send it with Nachum of Gamzu, because he has experienced many miracles."

He arrived at a certain inn to spend the night...During the night people in the inn arose and emptied the box of the treasure he had been carrying and filled it up with earth. When he discovered this next morning, he exclaimed, "This also is for the best."

When he arrived in Rome, they found that his bag was full of earth. The emperor said, "The Jews are mocking me by their gift. Put them to death!" Nachum again exclaimed, "This also is for the best!"

Whereupon Elijah appeared as one of them [a Roman] and said: "Perhaps this is some of the earth of their father Abraham, who threw earth [against his enemies] and it turned into swords!"

They threw some of this earth against a province that had

דער "גם זו לטובה" איז געווען אַ גוטער איד.

Der "gam zu l'tovah" iz gevehn a guter Yid.

[He who used to say] "this also is for the best" was a good Jew.

MEANING

An expression of admiration for the Jew trying to cope with his duty to justify every heavenly decree. Nachum of Gamzu was a good Jew who instilled encouragement, hope, and trust into the hearts of many, by showing through his own behavior that one must believe that everything God does is for the best.

Additionally, he must have been a good Jew, because it was not easy to justify the heavenly decrees that befell him as he did.

מיט שמחה גייט מען ארויס פון אלע ענגשאפטן.

Mit simcheh geit men arois fun alleh engshaften.

With joy one can overcome distress.

MEANING
Serving God with joy is strong enough to change one's decree for the better.

---

rebelled against the emperor and it turned into swords, enabling them to conquer the province.

They took him [Nachum] to the royal treasury, told him to fill his box with gold and to take it back to his Jewish brethren as a token of their appreciation.

(Yalkut Shimoni to Yeshayahu 41:1; also in Ta'anis 21a)

WORDS OF OUR SAGES
"For you will go out with joy..." (Yeshayahu 55:12) – With joy it is possible to come out of any trouble.
(R' Simchah Bunim of Przysucha)

IN THE SOURCES

A person cares less about losing money for which he did not toil. The Torah for which I studied hard has become fulfilled in me.
(Yalkut Koheles 965)

Every mitzvah for which Israel submitted to death during a royal ban...is still held firmly by them. However, every mitzvah for which Israel did not submit to death during a royal ban...is still weak in their hands. (Shabbos 130a)

WORDS OF OUR SAGES

He who makes friends easily will lose them easily.
(R' Shlomo ben Verga, Shevet Yehudah)

Why did Rebbi weep when he said, "One may acquire eternity in a single hour" (Avodah Zarah 10b)? – Because that which may be acquired in an hour may be lost in half an hour!
(R' Menachem Mendel of Kotzk)

"One who grasps quickly and forgets quickly, his gain is offset by his loss" (Avos 5:12) – for if he had toiled and not learned so quickly, he would not have forgotten so fast!
(Sefas Emes)

וואָס מ'באַקומט גיך
פֿאַרלירט מען גיך.

Vos m'bakumt gich farlirt men gich.

Easy come, easy go.

MEANING

The greater is the effort invested in acquiring something, the greater will be one's grip on it, and the precautions taken against its loss.

אַלצדינג דאַרף זיַין מיט אַ מאָס.

Altzding darf zein mit a moss.

Everything in the right measure.

MEANING

One must limit everything appropriately, and avoid acting carelessly.

WORDS OF OUR SAGES
*"Do not burn [as a fire offering] anything fermented or sweet" (Vayikra 2:11).
"Anything fermented" refers to someone who is utterly sour, day or night, weekday or Sabbath. "Anything sweet" refers to someone who is thoroughly sweet, to himself and others, at all times. Neither the fermented nor the sweet may come near to God. Rather, one must do everything in a measured way!*
(R' Shneur Zalman of Liadi, quoted in Sefer Ha-Toldos Maharash 75)

The Virtuous and Their Ways

B. SINCERE CHASIDIC DEVOUTNESS

אַז ס'איז אַ שטורעם אין דרויסן
מוז מען זיך אָנהאַלטן
אין רבין'ס גאַרטל.

Az s'iz a shturem in droissen
muz men zich onhalten in rebbin's gartel.

When it's stormy outside, hold on tightly to the Rebbe's belt.

EXPLANATION
Chasidim wear a gartel (cloth belt) for added sanctity. The Rebbe's belt, being especially holy, is worthy of serving as an instrument that can perform wonders.

MEANING
When a Jew's spiritual and physical safety is threatened, he must attach himself to holiness and purity. Such behavior is like holding onto a life preserver that enables one to survive.

IN TALES OF THE CHASIDIM
One summer day, R' Shmuel of Lelov was wearing his tallis and tefillin and studying in the Tykocin synagogue. Suddenly, a violent storm broke out. The Rebbe's assistant shook with fear.

"Hold on to my gartel," said the Rebbe, "and nothing will happen to you." That moment, lightning struck the wall of the synagogue, followed by a terrible noise. The wall cracked from top to bottom, and a fire broke out. The Rebbe and his assistant were not hurt.

WORDS OF OUR SAGES

Before the arrival of the Messiah, people's faith will be put to difficult tests. Whoever does not attach himself to the righteous of the generation will have great difficulty in maintaining his level of Jewish observance.
(Chiddushei Ha-Rim)

The Virtuous and Their Ways

וואָס שטאַרקער מ'האַלט זיך
אין רבין'ס גאַרטל,
אַלס מער וועט מען געהאָלפֿן.

Vos shtarker m'halt zich in rebbin's gartel, als mer vet men geholfen.

The tighter you hold on to the Rebbe's belt, the more will it help you.

MEANING
See previous saying.

WORDS OF OUR SAGES
The tzaddik represents "Jacob is the measure [lit., rope] of His inheritance" (Devarim 32:9): Just as one who holds one end of a rope and shakes it, causes the other to shake as well, such is the tzaddik – by connecting oneself to the tzaddik, the latter is immediately able to feel his problems and alleviate them.
("Divrei David" Chortkov, pp. 1-5)

אַן עצה פֿרעגט מען דעם רבין,
אַ ברכה קען מען נעמען
בײַ אַ גוטן פֿריינד אויך.

An eitza fregt men dem rebbin, a brocheh ken men nemmen bei a guten freind oich.

One seeks advice from the rabbi; a blessing from a good friend as well.

MEANING
See WORDS OF OUR SAGES section.

WORDS OF OUR SAGES
In Heaven, a friend's blessing is more important than the angel Gabriel's recommendation.
(R' Yisrael Ba'al Shem Tov)

It's true that one asks the rebbe for advice, and it's possible to receive a blessing from one's friend, but who is a chasid's best friend if not the rebbe?!
(Chasidic saying)

IN THE SOURCES

Everything the righteous do is done with Divine inspiration.
(Tanchuma Vayechi 14)

Since the day when the Temple was destroyed...although prophecy has been taken from the prophets, it has not been taken from the wise. (Bava Basra 12a) — *Although the prophets' prophecy, i.e., through apparitions and visions, has been taken away, the prophecy of the sages, which comes through wisdom, has not been taken away; they know the truth by divine inspiration.*
(Ramban ad loc.)

When a scholar comes to town, visit him, and accept all he says with awe and reverence, with fear and dread.
(Avos d'Rabbi Nasan 6:2)

Rabbi Meir said: "We may learn from a person's soul, for there is no one whose soul does not teach him every moment, yet the soul does not repeat things over and over."
(Chacham Ha-Razim quoting R' Pinchas of Korets)

Whoever thinks ill of his rabbi, it is as though he thinks ill of the Shechinah.
(Sanhedrin 110a)

פרעגסט אַ שאלה בײַ אַ רבין —
די ערשטע זאך איז רוח הקודש.
פרעגסטו איבער,
ענטפערט ער וואָס ער פאַרשטייט.
פרעגסטו נאָך אַ מאָל —
הערסטו וואָס דו ווילסט הערן.

Fregst a sh'eila bei a rebbin — di ershteh zach iz ru'ach ha-kodesh. Fregstu ibber, entfert er vos er farshteit. Fregstu noch a mol — herstu vos du vilst heren.

When you ask the rabbi a question, the first response has Divine inspiration. If you repeat the question, he answers according to his own understanding. If you ask again, you hear what you want to hear.

MEANING

Thanks to the special Heavenly assistance the rabbi receives, everything he says, from the very first word, points toward the truth. The more questions the questioner piles up — due to his lack of faith in the Divine inspiration behind the rabbi's words — the less worthy is he of obtaining a Divinely inspired answer. The response he does receive will correspond to his own spiritual state.

IN TALES OF THE CHASIDIM

A Chasid of R' Yosef Yitzchak of Lubavitch had to change his place of dwelling and was agonizing over where to move. He came to the Rebbe and listed the options before him with all their implications. The Rebbe then gave him his recommendation.

Upon leaving the Rebbe's office, the Chasid suddenly remembered a detail he had forgotten to share with him. After returning and telling it to the Rebbe, the latter said: "That additional information was superfluous. Neither does he who asks, nor he who answers, act alone. The questions are presented [at the outset] as they should be asked, and the answers, too, are given as they are supposed to be given!"

IN THE SOURCES

One must never speak in such a way as to give an opening to Satan.
(Berachos 19a)

"Is it shalom [well] with the boy?" She replied, "Shalom." (Melachim II, 4:26) – She did not want to say anything bad. (Although the boy had died, she refrained from saying it to Gehazi who had been sent by the prophet to inquire about his well-being.)
(Ralbag ad loc.)

בײַ אַ רבין מאַכט מען נישט שווער.

Bei a rebbin macht men nisht shver.

Don't exaggerate your problem to the rabbi.

MEANING

When presenting your problem to the rabbi, don't overstate it, so as "not to give an opening to Satan," and that you may "draw out" good utterances.

IN TALES OF THE CHASIDIM

When the eldest grandson of R' Yitzchak Isaac of Zidichov was seriously ill, his father, R' Sender Lippa, R' Isaac's eldest son, appealed to his father to pray for his ailing son. Not only did the illness, however, not abate, but it actually became worse, even to the point of endangering the boy's life.

A messenger was dispatched to again bring the patient to the attention of his holy grandfather, but R' Isaac was then closeted in his room and no one was permitted to interrupt him in his sacred work. His family finally decided to send to him his little grandson, Yehudah Tzvi, whom he adored. The child climbed the steps to his grandfather's room and, as he neared the door, he let out a cough.

Upon hearing the cough, the Rebbe opened the door and asked, "Nu?!"

The precocious child answered, "I came to tell you, Zeideh, that your grandson's condition is improving slowly, but you have to pray that he recover completely!"

The tzaddik's face lit up, and he hurried over to a cabinet from which he removed a handful of tea leaves. "Tell them to boil these leaves and have the patient drink the tea until he recuperates." Indeed, the sick boy's condition improved as he drank the tea, until he had completely recovered.

The next day, R' Sender Lippa came to inform his father that his son had gotten better. The tzaddik chastised him, saying: "You should learn some Chasidus from my little grandson, Yehudah Tzvi. Whereas you kept adding sorrow to my sorrow, that little boy knew how to revive my soul with good tidings. Thanks to him, the proper spirit rested upon me and enabled me to help bring about a complete recovery!"

אַן עצה פרעגט מען דעם רבין,
אַ ברכה בעט מען
בּײַ יעדען גוטן איד.

*An eitza fregt men dem rebbin,
a brocheh bet men bei yeden guten Yid.*

One seeks advice from the rabbi; any good Jew may be asked for a blessing.

MEANING
To give proper advice, one needs the Torah viewpoint and Heavenly assistance, which may be attained only by a person of great religious character, such as a rabbi. On the other hand, in order to bless others, one must really have their best interests at heart, something in which every good Jew excels.

IN THE SOURCES
He who takes the advice of sages will not falter.
(Shemos Rabbah 3:10)

Advice that manifests the word of God will last forever. (Yalkut Iyov 899)

Do not consider lightly the blessing of an ordinary person. (Berachos 7a)

WORDS OF OUR SAGES
When one invests, in his blessing of another, his mind, will, and desire, the blessing will come true.
(R' Menachem Mendel of Rymanow)

MAMMA USED TO SAY

WORDS OF OUR SAGES

Faith in Hashem purifies the soul; faith in the Sages purifies the body.
(R' Menachem Mendel of Vitebsk)

"They believed in Hashem and in Moshe, His servant – Then [they] sang..."
(Shemos 14:31; 15:1) – When they believed in Hashem and in Moshe, His righteous servant, they were privileged to sing about their deliverance.
(Chasidic saying)

אַז אַ איד גלייבט אין רבין העלפט דער אויבערשטער.

Az a Yid gleibt in rebbin helft der Oibershter.

When a Jew believes in the rabbi, God helps.

IN TALES OF THE CHASIDIM

R' Yisrael of Ruzhin related the following personal story:

A Jew who had leased a tavern was doing poorly financially and could not pay his landlord. He was warned that if he would not meet a final deadline, he would be thrown into jail. His wife, a true believer in great men of Torah, urged him to travel to and receive the blessing of the Ruzhiner Rebbe. When he refused, she herself made the trip. While waiting to see the Rebbe, she met a woman who had come to receive his blessing for her ill husband. Both women wrote their requests on slips of paper and gave them to the Rebbe's assistant.

Inadvertently, the assistant mixed up the Rebbe's responses: the assistant told the woman whose husband was ill that the Rebbe said God will help him, and he instructed the lease holder's wife to treat her husband with cupping-glasses. When she returned home, her husband burst out laughing at the Rebbe's advice: "I need money, not medical treatment," said he.

When the deadline for payment arrived, the woman implored her husband until he yielded to the suggested treatment, though he did not understand the meaning behind it. The tavern keeper lay in bed, the empty cupping-glasses placed on his back sucking in his flesh to the point of bleeding. Just then the landlord's servants arrived to rush the Jewish leaseholder off to their master. After seeing him in bed with a bloody blanket, they carried him off, bed and all.

"What happened to you?" asked the landlord with pitiful eyes. In a crying voice the lessee poured out his story: "Yesterday I went into the city to borrow money to pay you. Robbers jumped me on my way through the forest, beat me up and wounded me, and stole all my money. Now I am doubly in debt, to you, sir, and to my many creditors."

The landlord's compassion was aroused, and he immediately announced that since his tenant had been beaten because of him, he was revoking his debt as well as the rent for the next three years.

The Rebbe concluded his story: Upon receiving the woman's petition, I realized that I could not help her, so I prayed in a general way that God would support her. Of course, it never crossed my mind to recommend using cupping-glasses; my assistant did that inadvertently. It was the woman's simple trust in rabbis that brought her the deliverance! *(Ner Yisrael)*

C. A JEW'S VIRTUES

אַ אידישע נשמה קען מען נישט שאַצן.

A Yiddishe neshomeh ken men nisht shatzen.

A Jewish soul is invaluable.

MEANING
Reaction to a constructive act of a crude Jew.

אַ אידישן קרעכץ איז נישט צו שאַצן.

A Yiddishen krechtz iz nisht tzu shatzen.

The sigh of a Jew is invaluable.

MEANINGS
a. Even the sigh of a Jew has a spiritual dimension.
b. We must not mistreat one another, because "every Jewish sigh is heard on high."

IN THE SOURCES
The Jewish souls have been formed out of God's light. Even the distancing of His Shechinah in the world does not bring about the soul's separation from its Source, so that it remains connected to its primal source by a silver thread.
(Or Ha-Chaim, Bechukosai)

IN THE SOURCES
...and my sighing is not concealed from You.
(Tehillim 38:10)

WORDS OF OUR SAGES
How significant is the sigh of a Jew! A man who has a kosher butcher shop on one side of town and a non-kosher one on the other side, is busy commuting between the two on Friday. On the way, he passes by a synagogue and notices people who are already prepared for the Sabbath prayers. "Oy," he sighs. It is not the butcher in him that is sighing, it is the Jew in him! That is a Jewish sigh.
(R' Chanoch Henich of Alexander)

אַ אידישע קישקע איז נישט צו שאַצן.

A Yiddishe kishkeh iz nisht tzu shatzen.

A Jew's intestines are invaluable.

MEANING
Even the intestines, the most coarse part of the body, become refined and purified in the Jew's body by the myriad mitzvos he performs with them: abstention from forbidden foods and gluttony; hygienic care; eating on Sabbaths and festivals; eating matzah and maror; etc.

METAPHORICAL MEANING
Just as it is impossible to assess the value of one's intestines, because of its many twists and turns in the body, so it is impossible to appraise the worth of a Jew!

IN TALES OF THE CHASIDIM
R' Chaim of Tzanz was leaning back in bed following the Passover Seder, as he said: "Rejoice, my intestines, rejoice! How many 'names' [of God] there are in an olive-size piece of matzah, in maror, karpas, korech [the unleavened bread, bitter herbs, ritual vegetable, and 'sandwich' eaten during the Seder], in the four cups and festive meal of the holiday. And all these have entered into my bowels! Rejoice, O intestines, rejoice! How many 'names' are in you now!" Tears of joy flowed from his eyes.
(Mekor Chaim 99)

WORDS OF OUR SAGES
The Jew's body is so different from that of the gentile [due to the mitzvos performed with it], that only physicians who have special training in its particular characteristics should treat it.
(Chasam Sofer, Responsa)

א איד איז אַ גרויסער בעל-צדקה; פאַר אַ "גוט מארגן" גיט ער אָפ אַ "גוט יאר."

*A Yid iz a groisser baal tz'dokeh;
far a "gut morgen" git er op a "gut yor."*

A Jew is very generous: for a "good morning" he'll give you a "good year."

EXPLANATION
The saying relates to the accepted protocol regarding greetings among Yiddish speakers: one must respond to a greeter with a finer greeting than that which he received.

LEARNING FROM OUR SAGES
R' Yehonasan Eibeschutz used to hasten to greet enemies of the Jewish people. When queried, he explained that if said enemies were to greet him first with "Good morning," he would have to respond with "Good year," something he definitely did not wish.

IN THE SOURCES
He who occupies himself with the Torah for its own sake merits many things...Through him people benefit from counsel and wisdom, insight and strength. (Avos 6:1)

אַ איד אַ למדן גיט זיך אַן עצה.

A Yid a lamden git zich an eitza.

A learned Jew finds a way.

MEANING
Torah study provides the Jew with insight into all areas of life.

ווען זינגט אַ איד?
ווען ס'איז אים ביטער גוט.

Ven zingt a Yid? Ven s'iz im bitter gut.

When does a Jew sing? When things are very bitter for him.

MEANING
A Jew tries to be happy always: Even when in distress or pain (which occurs often), he accepts his afflictions with love and elevates himself through song toward the One Who provided them.

IN TALES OF THE CHASIDIM
When R' Yisrael of Modzhitz was hospitalized in Berlin, the surgeon who had operated on him told him: "I have just praised you before a German minister who is also here and does not stop screaming in pain. I told him: 'You should learn from the Jewish rabbi how to overcome your pain; he is suffering even more than you, yet he is relaxed and he sings.'"

R' Yisrael responded: "I too am screaming, but in order to save Jewish sounds from going to waste, I form them into songs and praises to the glory of God."

WORDS OF OUR SAGES
When the poet's heart becomes bitter, his poetry becomes sweet.
(R' Yedaya Ha-Bardashi)

The Virtuous and Their Ways

אידישער חן איז אומעטום שיין.

Yiddisher chein iz umetum shein.

Jewish grace is pleasing in every place.

> **IN THE SOURCES**
> "May God shine His countenance on you and be gracious to you."
> (Bemidbar 6:25) – May he bestow His grace onto you wherever you go.
> (Bemidbar Rabbah 11)
>
> A Jew is recognized wherever he goes.
> (Ibid., 16:15)

ווי אַ איד אין "אשרי"

Vi a Yid in "Ashrei"

Like a Jew saying "Ashrei"

EXPLANATION
A Jew recites "Ashrei yoshevei veisecha..." three times daily. Thus, he is very fluent in it.

METAPHORICAL MEANING
This describes someone who is very familiar with something.

> **IN THE SOURCES**
> Fortunate [Ashrei] are those who dwell in Your house...
> (Tehillim 84:5; recited together with Tehillim 144:15, 145:1-21 and 115:18)
>
> Whoever recites [the psalm] "Praise of David" [Tehillim 145] three times daily, is sure to inherit the world to come. (Berachos 4b)

Of and About Reality

OF AND ABOUT REALITY
ABOUT THIS AND THAT

געפּאַסט אַ הױקער צו דער װאַנט.

Gepasst a hoiker tzu der vant.

He fitted a hump to the wall.

MEANING
He tried to attach a hump, something inherently crooked, to a straight wall.

METAPHORICAL MEANING
Description of an action taken to try to match up two dissimilar things, for example, an innately curved object and a straight one, or someone who is faint-hearted with a group of stubborn people, etc.

דער װאָס האָט אַ הױקער מוז אים טראָגן.

Der vos hot a hoiker muz im troggen.

He who has a hump must bear it.

METAPHORICAL MEANING
He who has a problem must either tackle it or resign himself to it.

גענייטע זאַכען טרענען זיך.

Geneiteh zachen trennen zich.

Stitched clothes are likely to become undone.

(Forced actions do not endure.)

EXPLANATION

The Yiddish "geneiteh" has two meanings: 1) sewn together; 2) forced. The saying is directed at both.

MEANING

Forced actions – those done not according to one's choosing, but under duress – are like stitched fabrics: their joining together is precarious, and they are likely to come apart.

מ'זאָל אַלץ צום גוטן אויסלייגן.

M'zol altz tzum guten oisleigen.

Try to solve everything for the good.

INSTRUCTION

Think only positively, and bite your tongue (lit., "never speak in a way that will give an opening to Satan").

Of and About Reality

וואו ס'איז איבעריג דארט פעלט.

Vu s'iz ibberig dort felt.

Where there's extra, there's a lack.

(Overdoing is underachieving.)

MEANING

Wholeness implies that there is nothing either too much or too little. If there is something extra, there may also be a deficiency.

IN THE SOURCES

Every addition [of a limb] is equal to the loss [of a limb] (both make an animal unfit). (Hullin 58b)

WORDS OF OUR SAGES

"You are One" – Your unity can bear neither deduction nor addition, neither deficiency nor augmentation.
(R' Shelomo ben Gevirol)

א טויבער האט געהערט,
ווי א שטומער האט דערציילט,
אז א בלינדער האט אליין געזען,
ווי א קרומער איז געלאפן...

A toiber hot gehert, vi a shtummer hot dertzeilt, az a blinder hot alein gezehn, vi a krummer iz geloffen...

A deaf person heard a mute telling about a blind person who saw a lame one running...

METAPHORICAL MEANING

Description of an exaggerator's stories.

IN THE SOURCES

(A source for the combination of characters:) Then the eyes of the blind will be uncovered, and the ears of the deaf will be opened. Then the lame will leap like a gazelle, and the tongue of the mute will sing. (Yeshayahu 35:5, 6)

IN THE SOURCES

From the time of Moses until Rebbi.... From the time of Rebbi until R. Ashi there was no one who was supreme both in Torah and in worldly affairs.
(Gittin 59a)

Not everyone is privileged to enjoy two tables [scholarship and wealth].
(Berachos 5b)

WORDS OF OUR SAGES

The Divine Wisdom apportioned various criteria (poverty, wealth, health, illness, etc.) with which to try people, as it saw fit and proper. Thus, each human being has a particular part in the test...and will be rewarded according to his actions under his particular circumstances.
(Ramchal, Derech Hashem II: 3)

אַלץ אין איינעם
איז נישטאָ בײַ קיינעם.

Altz in einem iz nishto bei keinem.

No one has it all.
(Nobody is perfect.)

MEANING
No one has a monopoly on merits or accomplishments. Everyone has his own portion in the world.

יעדער טעפל האָט זײַן דעקל.

Yeder teppel hot zein deckel.

Every pot has its cover.
(For every Jack there's a Jill.)

METAPHORICAL MEANING
There exists a suitable mate (or friend) for every person; every problem has an appropriate solution, etc.

Of and About Reality

אַ געזונטן קאָפּ אין אַ קראַנקן בעט

A gezunten kop in a kranken bet

A healthy head in a sickbed

METAPHORICAL MEANING

Bewilderment: Why needlessly get into a situation that begs for trouble?

Alternatively, this is an exclamation in response to a complication that has arisen due to one's unnecessary involvement in something.

IN THE SOURCES

He put his head into an empty noose. (Metaphorically: He got himself into trouble for nothing.)
(Yerushalmi, Nedarim 1:9)

He is carrying his own gallows (digging his own grave). (Metaphorically: He is bringing about his own death.) (Bereshis Rabbah 56)

דאָרט וואוּ די הינט בילן, דאָרט איז דאָ אַ יִשוּב.

Dort vu di hint billen, dort iz do a yishuv.

The barking of dogs means a community is nearby.

METAPHORICAL MEANING

Loud criticism attests to the importance of the subject under criticism.

IN THE SOURCES

This will be a sign for you: If you see a cemetery, know that you are nearing a city.
(Yalkut Tehillim 680)

אַ פַּאַרך מיט געקרייזלטע האָר?!

A parch mit gekreizelteh hor?!

A bald head with curly hair?!

METAPHORICAL MEANING

Description of a paradox or an impossibility.

IN THE SOURCES
Oil, even when mixed with any other liquid, will rise above them.
(Shemos Rabbah 36:1)

אמת קומט ארויס
ווי בוימל אויפן וואסער.

Emes kumt arois vi boimel oifen vasser.

Truth emerges like oil on water.

METAPHORICAL MEANING
The truth will eventually come out.

IN THE SOURCES
A pearl is a pearl wherever it may be. (Megillah 15a)

WORDS OF OUR SAGES
A Jew must be treated as a golden dinar: his light shines even when he is found in mud or dung. All you have to do is lift him up, wash him and polish him, and he will shine as he used to.
(R' Mordechai of Lechovitz)

גאָלד לייכט ארויס פון די בלאָטע.

Gold leicht arois fun di blotteh.

Gold glitters even in the mud.

METAPHORICAL MEANING
The positive stands out [even] in a negative environment; truth emanates [even] from the falsehood in which it is mired.

די זעלביגע יענטע,
נאָר אַנדערש געשלײַערט.

Di zelbigeh yenteh, nor andersh geshleiert.

The same yenteh,
but with a different veil.
(Same thing, different face.)

METAPHORICAL MEANING
Reaction to a change on the outside that did not affect the inside; the essence or reality did not change, only the way it was presented changed.

נישט דערגאַנגען, נישט דערפאָרן.

Nisht dergangen, nisht derforen.

He neither walked nor rode.

MEANING
He was immobilized.

METAPHORICAL MEANING
Description of someone who was in a situation that deprived him of all courses of action, because they were conflictive or contradictory.

אַ נײַער מלך, נײַע גזירות

A neier melech, neieh g'zeiros

A new king, new decrees

MEANING

A cry of distress in reaction to a new era that ushers in new restrictions and requirements.

IN THE SOURCES

"Now there arose a new king..." (Shemos 1:8) – His decrees were new. (Sotah 11a)

מ'דרייט זיך און מ'פרייט זיך.

M'dreit zich un m'freit zich.

They go around and celebrate.

MEANING

Description of the way of idlers: they are happy doing nothing.

צו גוט איז אויך נישט גוט.

Tzu gut iz oich nisht gut.

Too good is also no good.

MEANING

Reaction to an effort to attain perfection where it is not applicable: Goodness is complete; "too good" detracts from the completeness, because it comes at the expense of other important values.

IN THE SOURCES

"Don't be overly righteous." (Koheles 6:16)

Whoever adds, detracts. (Sanhedrin 29a)

An extra [limb] is the same as a missing [limb]. (Too much is also a deficiency.) (Chullin 58b)

אַלע מעלות איז דער גרעסטער חסרון.

Alleh mailes iz der grester chissoren.

To have all merits is the greatest drawback.

MEANING

An expression, usually of grief or sorrow, concerning the bad luck that accompanies virtuous people and "perfect" things.

IN THE SOURCES

R. Yehudah said in the name of Shemuel: "Why did the kingdom of Shaul not endure? – Because he had no blemish." *(Yoma 22b)*

אַ חסרון, די כלה איז צו שיין!

A chissoren, di kalleh iz tzu shein!

A liability, the kallah is too beautiful!

(A spoilsport will complain that the bride is too pretty.)

MEANING

A protest against inappropriate criticism – such as finding something wrong with a bride's looks, when everyone agrees that her beauty is one of her assets.

IN THE SOURCES

(Beis Hillel said that when dancing before a bride, one should say:) "Beautiful and graceful bride." *(Kesubos 17a)*

עס טהוט זיך אויף טישן און אויף בענק...

Es tut zich oif tishen un oif benk...

It's happening on tables and benches...

(Things are all out of whack/in disarray.)

METAPHORICAL MEANING

Description of something done in a haphazard or improvised manner.

די גענצע וועלט איז ווי אַ חלום.

Di gantzeh velt iz vi a cholem.

The whole world is like a dream.

MEANINGS

a. An attempt, in a pessimistic vein, to diminish the value of physical occurrences in this world.
b. Criticism of the tendency to overestimate the importance of materialism: Of what benefit is it, if the whole world will fly away like a dream?!

IN THE SOURCES

...will fly away like a dream.
(Iyov 20:8)

Of and About Reality

די גאַנצע וועלט איז ווי אַ חלום,
נאָר בעסער אַ גוטער חלום
איידער אַ שלעכטער.

*Di gantzeh velt iz vi a cholem,
nor besser a guter cholem eider a shlechter.*

The whole world is like a dream, but a good dream is better than a nightmare.

MEANING
A mocking response to the preceding saying, emphasizing the "benefits" of transitory life to those who are living it.

מײַן נשמה
איז אויך נישט קיין ראָזשינקע.

Mein neshomeh iz oich kein rozhinkeh.

My soul is also not a raisin.

MEANING
Someone claiming his basic rights uses this as an explanation and justification: My soul also comes from God, and is not to be treated indifferently.

IN THE SOURCES

A custom invalidates a law.
(Yerushalmi, Yevamos 12:1; Bava Metzi'a 7:1)

People follow the procedure that no law is instituted until it becomes a custom. Regarding the Sages' statement that "a custom invalidates a law," it applies to a custom of the pious men of old. A custom that has no support from the Torah, however, is merely like an error of judgment. (Soferim 14:18)

אַ מנהג ברעכט אַ דין.

A minhag brecht a din.

A custom overrides a law.

MEANING
A custom has great force,
as even a law may depend on it.

METAPHORICAL MEANING
Observing a custom can be powerful: sometimes in its merit divine justice crumbles and turns into divine mercy.

ביז צו די קרעטשמע דאַרף מען אויך אַ טרונק בראָנפֿן.

Biz tzu di kretshmeh darf men oich a trunk bronfen.

One needs a drink of brandy even before reaching the tavern.

METAPHORICAL MEANING
We must find a temporary solution to the problem until it is ultimately resolved.

גיב נישט אומגעבעטענע עצות!

Gib nisht umgebeteneh eitzos!

Don't give unsolicited advice!

INSTRUCTION
Some offerings are helpful only when needed. Offering advice is one of them.

IN THE SOURCES
A person who is exempt from doing something, but does it anyway, is called an ignoramus.
(Yerushalmi, Berachos 2:9; Shabbos 1:2)

זַיי נישט קיין "וצדקתך" איד.

Zei nisht kein "vetzidkas'cha" yid.

Don't be a "vetzidkas'cha" [of your righteousness] Jew.

MEANING
Don't be overly righteous: don't adopt stringencies that are incompatible with your position.

IN THE SOURCES
...Your bountifulness they will express, and of Your righteousness they will joyfully sing. (Satirically: Don't do things only in order that people talk about how good you are and "joyfully sing of your righteousness.")
(Tehillim 145:7)

אַן אויבער חכם

An oiber chochom

He's too smart [for his own good].
(He's Mister Know-it-all.)

MEANING
Description of a wiseacre – one who thinks he is smart, and acts accordingly, while he really is not.

IN THE SOURCES
Some increased their knowledge to their own detriment: Doeg and Achisofel.
(Koheles Rabbah 1:39)

The wise man knows that his knowledge is limited; the fool thinks he knows everything.
(Ba'alei Ha-Mussar)

Of and About Reality

שטאַרק ווי דער גוײשער גאָט

Shtark vi der goyisher gott

As strong as the heathen's god

METAPHORICAL MEANING
Description of something insignificant.

IN THE SOURCES
Their idols are silver and gold, the handiwork of man. They have a mouth but cannot speak; they have eyes but cannot see. They have ears but cannot hear; they have a nose but cannot smell. (Tehillim 115:4-6)

Since idolatry is inconsequential, why are idols called "gods"? – To give credit to all who renounce idolatry. (Devarim Rabbah 2:11)

ווענט האָבן אויערן, גאַסן האָבן אויגן.

Vent hobben oiren, gassen hobben oigen.

Walls have ears; streets have eyes.

METAPHORICAL MEANING
This is a warning to one who has a secret: Secrets are apt to become revealed by someone listening to things said in private, or by someone observing one's actions in public.

IN THE SOURCES
Walls have ears. (Vayikra Rabbah Ch. 32)

The stones and the beams of a man's house testify against him, as it is said (Chavakuk 2:11): "For a stone will cry out of the wall, and a sliver will answer it from a beam." (Chagigah 16a)

Of and About Reality

בײַ אַ סך באַלעבאָסטעס
גייט די שטוב אויף רעדער.

Bei a sach balebostes geit di shtub oif reder.

Too many housewives will make a mess (lit., "will make the house go on wheels").

(Too many cooks spoil the broth.)

METAPHORICAL MEANING
If many partners are involved in the business, disorder is likely to set in.

IN THE SOURCES
A pot of two partners [cooks] is neither hot nor cold. (Eruvin 3a)

די אומריינע פֿאַר די ריינע,
גיסט נישט אַרוים!

Di umreineh far di reineh, gist nisht arois!

Don't pour out the dirty before you have the clean!

(A bird in the hand is worth two in the bush.)

METAPHORICAL MEANING
Don't renounce what you already have, though it may be imperfect, for something better that is still only a wish.

IN THE SOURCES
Destruction by old men is construction. (Megillah 31b)

נייען און טרענען דאַרף מען קענען.

Neien un trennen darf men kennen.

One must know how to sew and how to rip.

MEANING
To make a proper garment, one must know how to sew. One must also know how to tear apart what needs to be altered.

METAPHORICAL MEANING
Not only actions require wisdom and knowledge: so does nullifying or repealing them.

בעסער אַ מיאוסע לאַטע אײדער אַ שײנער לאָך.

Besser a mi'useh latteh eider a sheiner loch.

Better to have an ugly patch than a pretty hole.

(Half a loaf is better than none.)

METAPHORICAL MEANING
A partial, though imperfect, solution to a problem is better than no solution at all.

Of and About Reality

בעסער גוט און אַ ביסל,
איידער שלעכט און אַ פולע שיסל.

*Besser gut un a bissel,
eider shlecht un a fulleh shissel.*

Better good and a little,
than bad and a lot.

(It's quality, not quantity,
that counts!)

MEANING
It is worth giving up quantity for quality.

דעם שעפ פון באד גיט מען נישט אוועק.

Dem shep fun bod git men nisht aveck.

One does not give away the bathhouse cup.

METAPHORICAL MEANING
Don't disdain essential objects, even if they are not worth much.

IN THE SOURCES

Better a dish of vegetables where there is love than a fattened ox where there is hatred. (Mishlei 15:17)

Better dry bread and peacefulness with it than a house full of meals eaten in strife. (Mishlei 17:1)

Better one hot pepper than a whole basket of pumpkins. (Yoma 85a)

מער ווי צוויי פאַר אַ גראָשן.

Mer vi tzvei far a groshen.

[It's worth] more than "two for a penny."

EXPLANATION

Merchants used to assess the value of merchandise according to the number of items of that commodity that were worth a groshen.

METAPHORICAL MEANING

A "commercial" description of something that is not cheap.

זאל זיין פון קוזק – א בי צום לעבן.

Zol zein fun Kozak – a bi tzum leben.

Let it come from a Cossack – as long as it can revive.

MEANING

An expression used by a person who has to resort to a source upon which he would prefer not to rely: Since it is vital to my existence, I won't be so choosy about where I get it.

אז די קאץ איז נישטא – טאנצן ארום די מייז.

Az di katz iz nishto – tantzen arum di meiz.

When the cat is away, the mice dance.

METAPHORICAL MEANING
When the threat or the constraining power is removed, everyone reverts to doing what comes naturally, or as they please.

מ'דארף אויף דעם א קופערנעם יצר הרע.

M'darf oif dem a kupernem yetzer hara.

It requires an evil inclination of copper.

MEANING
A description of something earthly for which people generally have a craving, but which, in this particular case, will not give pleasure, or will be very hard to attain. Therefore, it will require an unusually strong ("like copper") evil impulse to try and attain it in any way possible.

געקניפט און געבונדן

Geknipt un gebunden

Tied and bound

METAPHORICAL MEANING
Description of something made up of various components that are tied and bound (and entangled) with each other.

פון א יא און פון א ניין און פון א נישט

Fun a yo un fun a nein un fun a nisht

Of a "yes," a "no," and a "not"

METAPHORICAL MEANING
Description of something made up of all possibilities.

יעדער שטעקן האט צוויי העקן.

Yeder shtecken hot tzvei hecken.

Every stick has two ends.

METAPHORICAL MEANING
There are opposing sides to everything. (There are two sides to every story.)

Of and About Reality

"נח" מיט זיבן גרייזן
"Noach" mit zibben greizen
"Noach" spelled with seven mistakes

EXPLANATION
It is unusual to write the name "Noach" [נח] wrong, as it has only two letters; how much more so with seven mistakes!

METAPHORICAL MEANING
Description of an action performed with as many mistakes as possible.

אויב ס׳איז דא שניי קען מען מאַכן גאָמלקעס.
Oib s'iz do shnei ken men machen gommelkes.
You can make snowballs only when there is snow.

METAPHORICAL MEANING
You can't make something out of nothing. In order for a blessing to take effect, it must be applied to something that exists.

IN THE SOURCES

Straw is not given...and they tell us to make bricks!
(Shemos 5:15, 16)

And Elisha said to her: "...Go, borrow vessels for yourself...." And he [her son] said to her, "There is not another vessel," and the oil stopped.
(Melachim II, 4:2-7)

༼ MY MOTHER — IN LOVING MEMORY ༽

"Mamma used to say..."
"Back in Warsaw they used to say..."
"People ['the world'] say..."
"It says in the holy books..."

It was with these opening words that my mother, ע"ה, would unlock the "jewel box" that was filled with her wonderful gems and treasures. That box did not contain golden jewelry inlaid with precious stones, nor did it hold glittering coins or other valuables. It was Mother's spiritual possessions that were concealed there, and their radiance illuminated all who were close to her.

My mother had "an understanding heart [that] acquires knowledge" (*Mishlei* 18:15) — a heart full to overflowing with wisdom she absorbed in her parents' home, wisdom that became enriched by her life experience.

She was nourished from the wellsprings of eternity in the home of her father, R' Yehudah Leib Freibaum, הי"ד, a Chasid and leader, learned and of good family. Their home was filled with goodness and kindness, steeped in the effervescent Chasidic life of Warsaw.

Mother had the good fortune of fulfilling the words of our Sages: "the wife of a scholar is like a scholar" (*Shevuos* 30b), when she married my esteemed father and teacher, the Gaon Rabbi Yaakov Chanoch Sankevitz, זצ"ל, who taught at Yeshivas Sefas Emes in Jerusalem. She was a true helpmate to him, standing by his side for over forty years.

Their home served as a meeting place for great Torah personalities and Chasidic leaders, and as a warm retreat for the yeshiva students, who became very attached to it. It was in the recesses of that home, whose very walls were saturated with Torah and holiness, that my mother's character expanded greatly.

She herself did all she could to increase and amplify her spiritual assets, and to turn them into tools with which to carry out the sacred tasks of a Jewish wife and mother. She often read Yiddish translations of holy works, such as *Ein Yaakov*, *Nachalas Tzvi*, and *Menoras Ha-Maor*. Much of what she learned she knew by heart, and she frequently quoted Scriptural verses, sayings of the Sages, and stories about the righteous. My father, זצ"ל, was referring to her when he said that some "members of his family" are eloquent even in front of scholars!

My mother did not acquire her wisdom at school or seminary, for she had attended neither. She imbibed it directly from her spiritual surroundings and from her rich experience. Her wisdom was attained from life itself; she was therefore able to pave our way through life with paths of wisdom.

* * *

Mamma's sayings were like pearls of choice wisdom, inlaid in a frame of pure speech, unblemished, pristine, and genuine. They shine from having been immersed in the purifying waters of her burning faith.

She had the astuteness to be able to find the saying that was most appropriate for every time, place, and situation. "Every saying has its place," she used to say, and she intelligently wove her aphorisms into her talk and actions for the benefit of those around her, to enlighten and guide them.

Her pearls of wisdom were wonderful in their variety and adaptability: Some served as remedies, bringing sweetness to bitter times, spicing up routine with stimulating flavors, or calming turbulence. Some served as a *tzohar* (the luminous stone that lit up Noah's ark), providing a beacon of encouragement and joy, dispelling dark clouds from the heart. Others were like jewels whose very beauty bring delight.

Some were like flintstones, igniting the fire of excitement and enthusiasm for change and improvement. Some were like an *even ezer*, helping through good advice; or an *even ha-ezel*, guiding travelers to their desired destination. It was remarkable how they were able to influence listeners differently, each according to what he or she was able and willing to receive.

Mamma's sayings were woven into the fabric of her life. One could say that her deeds exceeded her wisdom, the latter having been expressed through words only after the former had become apparent. In other words — she preached what she practiced!

Perhaps this was the secret behind the special flavor her sayings had, a flavor that remained fresh and precious to her family and many friends and acquaintances even years after her passing. We can sense how she remarkably integrated wisdom and action if we look at some of her behavior.

Frequently, after the conclusion of events and issues that seemed very important to the people involved, Mother, ה״ע, would put things in the right perspective by saying, "The sum of the matter, when all is said and done, is: learn Torah, serve the Creator, and fear no one."

How fitting for her were those words, for they typified her whole life, a rich life that spanned eighty-seven years. What was remarkable about my mother was the flawless consistency in her behavior. Despite her having lived through a most difficult and turbulent period in the history of our people, a period that caused many good people to change their priorities in life, she remained true to her faith and did not change her ways. Her dedication to my father's Torah study was boundless. She never flinched at all from facing the many difficulties and trials that faced her.

* * *

Love of Torah filled my mother's entire being and served as her main delight. Being the daughter of merchants, she liked to measure the Torah in business terms: "Torah is the best merchandise!" she used to say. She steered her life accordingly, encouraging everyone she met to acquire more Torah knowledge.

She had a great and decisive share in my esteemed father's Torah. He had been one of the primary movers in the rebuilding of the Torah world in Eretz Yisrael over seventy years ago. He played a central and pioneering role in the history of Yeshivos there, and my mother deserves much of the credit.

To enable him to fulfill this task, she gave up the pleasures they had enjoyed while living in her father's home, close to both of their dedicated families in Poland, and followed him to Eretz Yisrael. Here she became acquainted with poverty, and she raised her children with *yisurim shel ahavah* — "afflictions of love."

Her trials and tribulations did not dampen her perpetual joy of being a helpmate to her esteemed husband. Rather, she said, "Even dry bread in the Holy Land tastes like dough kneaded with oil, like the manna that fell for our ancestors in the wilderness, to which no delicacy in the world could compare."

* * *

During the days of mourning for my father, זצ"ל, among the consolers was a man who had been one of the first students of Yeshivas Sefas Emes. He recalled the following instructive story:

> As soon as the Rosh Yeshivah began his lecture, he would become totally immersed in it. Every day, about an hour into the lesson, the Rebbetzin would bring him a cup of warm milk mixed with honey. She worried about his health, and this helped to strengthen his voice, that became hoarse during the heated Torah discussion. One cold winter day, she came as usual and stood outside the window holding his cup of milk, waiting for her husband to take it as usual. It was

snowing and bitterly cold. Inside sat the rav, engrossed in a deep Talmudic discussion, face aglow and completely oblivious to his surroundings. She continued to stand there, shivering, respectfully holding the rapidly cooling cup of milk in her slowly freezing hands.

The students, noticing that the Rebbetzin had been standing outside a long time, tried to signal the fact to the Rosh Yeshivah — but to no avail. He was so absorbed in his lesson that he did not notice their gestures. Considering the situation an emergency, all the students closed their Gemaras in unison! Their Rebbe then looked up from his own Gemara in confusion, and immediately realized what was happening. He quickly rose and hurried to the window to take the cup of milk his righteous Rebbetzin had brought.

The student who told this story compared the Rosh Yeshivah's home to that of Rabbi Akiva, who said about his wife Rachel, "All that I and you [my students] have, is due to her."

Upon hearing that, my mother said modestly: "*Nu*, the combination of husband and wife is like a 'one' and a 'zero.' " She considered herself to be like that "zero," whose value increases only when it stands next to something of value.

Indeed, when eulogizing her, the *Penei Menachem* declared: "She deserves that it be said of her what the *Tanna* Rabbi Akiva said about his wife: 'Mine and yours is hers!' "

* * *

Mother would prolong her praying. She regarded prayer as a gift and a privilege to be utilized. She especially entreated at length for her children and encouraged other women who were close to her to do so as well, saying, "A mother should pray." No one knows like a mother knows what the family needs. No one takes their needs to heart like a mother can. Therefore if she invests all her strength praying and supplicating for them — surely she will be answered!

She also knew from experience how difficult proper prayer could be, due to a mother's many ongoing responsibilities. Accordingly, she reasoned: "It is better to stand by the pot and think about the prayer-book [that is, pray], than to stand by the prayer-book and have the pot in mind."

In her old age she often sat by the window at home, holding her worn-out *Siddur* or her *Sefer Tehillim*, whose pages had become bent and yellow from use. Her lips moved incessantly and her eyes were filled with tears. This she continued to do even in her final years, when her eyesight was so poor that she could hardly see the letters. Then it seemed like the letters saw her... As she passed her finger over the words of prayer, they appeared to be jumping into her mouth by themselves, without first going through her eyes...

Sometimes she would stop for a moment, and turn to God as a daughter turns to her father, saying, "Master of the Universe, I am Yours and You are mine — 'I am my Beloved's and my Beloved is mine' — please accept my prayer as if it were said word by word."

*   *   *

My mother, ה"ע, utilized thanks as well. She warmly thanked God for everything that happened to her, good or "bad," recognizing with conviction that whatever God decreed must be good. She never complained, despite her many hardships. Her heart overflowed with only appreciation to God, Whom she blessed with her every breath. "May the One Who dwells above be blessed and praised," was what she always said and requested others to say. In trying times, too, she strengthened herself in perfect faith, saying, "Whatever God does is surely good!"

Every morning upon awakening, she recited *Modah ani* with the thrill and joy of one who has just recovered from a serious illness and who was therefore thanking God for having given him life as a gift. While saying her prayers, when she came to the words *Modim anachnu lach* [We thank You], she was almost in tears. She regarded God's kindnesses to her with deep-rooted faith and a strong love, and would frequently say: "We don't even realize what we have to be thankful to God for."

She constantly believed in the goodness to come and looked forward to it every day. "Man lives with hope," she would say, "because everything comes from God, and He never neglects us." No wonder, then, that she was always smiling with the true joy of one who merits serving the good and beneficent God. This shone forth from her eyes and radiated out onto everything around her.

My mother was renowned for her love of the Jewish people. She loved every single Jew, for they are all called "children of God," and whoever loves the Father and perceives His goodness, loves and draws near His children as well.

People enjoyed visiting her, and she did all she could to make them happy. She would prepare many kinds of homemade delicacies and urge her guests to partake of them, saying, "Please don't leave my home without making a blessing!" She would spare no effort in making their visit pleasurable. When she was complimented for the tastiness of her food, she would say, "The cholent's success depends on the guests who eat it."

She remembered the mailman and the sanitation worker as well, hurrying to offer them cold drinks in the summer and hot ones in winter. She also gave them generous gifts before the holidays.

Many poor people frequented my mother's home. They found there an attentive ear for their troubles, and wisdom for solving their problems. She listened to them with infinite patience, shared their sorrows, and sighed with them over their suffering. She used to say: "If you can't help with money, at least you should help with a sigh."

She tried to help them assuage their guilt for having made mistakes, by saying, "A person is only a person." She raised their hopes for a better future with, "Where there are thorns, there a rose will grow." Sometimes she convinced them that, "Things can get no worse," or "When things get so bad, salvation must be near."

She would often offer people blessings that flowed from her warm heart and pure lips, blessings that attested to their having come from one who was rooted in her tradition and was the wife of a scholar. To someone who was worried about the future she would say, "May good angels watch over you." She would wish a child, "May you grow up and be happy." If someone complained because of too few family celebrations, she would pray while seeing that person to the door, "Master of the Universe, may we merit to drink 'L'chaim' at Your children's happy occasions."

Even after my father, ז"ל, passed away, Mamma made sure that her home remained open to the hungry and the sufferer and that guests always continued to feel welcome in it. She invariably tried to make her guests feel that their visit gave her great pleasure and that they had performed a big mitzvah. "You have earned a great mitzvah," she would say. "May we be able to reciprocate at your celebrations."

When someone would bless her in return, she would reply humbly, "From your mouth straight to God's ears," or she would sigh softly and say to herself, "We should deserve to see this blessing come true!"

* * *

It is impossible to accurately describe Mamma's diligence and joy in performing the mitzvos, and the caring and sensitivity she displayed toward them.

She constantly urged us not to miss the opportunity to perform a mitzvah, especially one that people tended to neglect. "Children," she would say, "mitzvos are lying around on the ground — you only have to bend down to pick them up!" One could discern her exceeding love for the mitzvos, for example, even from the way she lovingly cleaned around the mezuzah every day, ensuring that it would be esthetic before God.

MY MOTHER — IN LOVING MEMORY

My mother spared no effort in giving charity. Many needy people came to see her on Rosh Chodesh and before Festivals, and she gave to the best of her ability. When she went out, she gave to every poor person asking for charity whom she met, explaining: "It's hard to determine who is really in need, but if you give to many, you're bound to get someone who is truly needy." In a similar vein, she would say, "A person must be in the habit of giving."

As the daughter of Chasidim and the wife of a Chasid, my mother clung to the words of Tzaddikim with perfect faith, simplicity, and submission, following their guidance in every matter, large or small. She would say, "The tighter you hold on to the Rebbe's belt, the greater will be your salvation." She often spoke about the need for such trust in troubled times such as these, the days before the arrival of *Mashiach*. "During these turbulent times, one must hold on to the Rebbe's *gartel*," she proclaimed — and she did.

My mother's sayings created around her a perpetual educational atmosphere. She was our mentor, broadening our horizons, warding off provincialism and narrow-mindedness.

I remember one of my visits to her with my baby daughter. Mamma had a pensive look on her face as she watched her little granddaughter run around. Suddenly she smiled and said, "My mother used to say that we can learn three things from children: They are never idle, they are always happy, and when they need something they cry out to their father!" In other words, one must learn something from every situation.

Once, when I shared with my mother some of my worries about the future, she said in a dismissive tone, "R' Mendele of Worka already said: Let's not worry about what tomorrow will bring; better to fix the present and the past." Those words were enough to remind me where I ought to invest my time and energy.

She had no need for harsh moralizing; her sayings were enough, enabling the hearer to accept what was said without feeling hurt and with no need to be defensive or apologetic. Her dignified manner inspired serenity, so that all who approached her felt a need to improve their behavior.

*   *   *

The years of a person's old age are usually years of diminishing strength and vitality; one becomes more dependent on society and less able to contribute to it. This can lead one to feel that his life is a burden, for himself and those around him.

This was not true in the case of my mother, who merited to live a long life. Despite her diminishing strength and failing eyesight, she was happy for every day of her life. She called her later years "the years given as a gift," referring to them as if they were a bonus, and she always thanked God for them. "I want to live," she would say, "for 'the dead cannot praise God'!"

She conscientiously used those years to prepare herself for the transition to the next world. "I don't want to be ashamed in this world," she would say, "or humiliated in the next. No one lives forever; we must prepare for the feast." She prayed often for the following: "Master of the Universe, may I be able to serve You and take care of myself with a clear mind"; that is, "not to be a burden on — or need — anyone, but You!"

My mother had the merit to be granted her wish by Heaven. Although she weakened considerably in her last days, she did not heed her doctors' recommendations to be transferred to the hospital. "Do you see that old cupboard in my room?" she asked her worried family. "As long as it is here, it is whole. As soon as you move it, however, it will come apart and no longer be able to serve its function. When you move old furniture from its place, it comes apart. I would like to meet the angel of death in my own bed."

And so, on the evening of the holy Sabbath, *Parashas Ha-Chodesh*, 5747 (1987), after reciting the *Shehakol* blessing over a glass of water, possessing a clear mind and a good name, she returned her pure soul to her Maker. May her soul be bound up in the bond of everlasting life.

*   *   *

The seven days of mourning passed. The death of my mother caused a great emptiness in me, which continued to widen and deepen as I became more and more aware of the enormity of my loss. I had become orphaned of a loving and dedicated mother whose magnanimity, nobility, and integrity added immeasurably to her love and devotion to her family.

Moreover, I had lost the pillar of fire that had illuminated my way in life, that guided, led, and directed me on the right path with the flame of burning faith. I had lost also the pillar of cloud that had removed all obstacles in the wilderness of life, and that had cushioned all difficulties with comforting and encouraging words, thus infusing the future with hope.

I felt so lonely without my mother, who had been steeped in a deeply rooted Jewish tradition. My thirst for her words of wisdom — which had been to us as refreshing as living waters to branches and leaves — intensified with each passing day...

*   *   *

MY MOTHER — IN LOVING MEMORY

Saturday night — the shining stars remind us that it is time to part from the Sabbath Queen and to cross over to the work week. I gaze at the stars helplessly, knowing that I must prepare for the coming week, but lacking the strength to do so.

When Mother was alive, I would go to her house with my children every Shabbos afternoon for *Se'udah Shelishis*, the third Sabbath meal. It was then that we experienced the pleasant and uplifting hours of *Ra'ava d'Ra'avin* (God's special favor) in the company of our mother and grandmother.

After *Havdalah*, it was time to depart. As she escorted us out, Mother would lovingly shower us with blessings for the new week: "Take a big bundle of blessings for a big week"; "Whatever you do, and wherever you turn, may God grant you principal with interest!"

Sometimes she would wish us: "May you find favor in the eyes of God and man," or "The *Mashiach* is already among us; may you merit seeing him." She would kiss her grandchildren warmly, bestowing on them the Jewish grandmother's blessing, "May you grow and flourish!" She also made them feel as if they had done her a favor by visiting her, saying, "May your children do the same for you in your old age."

Now and then she would add a package of helpful advice for the coming week: "Don't busy yourself with achieving, just with doing"; "Always remember: No one does anything alone"; or, "Always be happy, for happiness takes us out of any distress."

My mother's words were like refreshing dew, restoring in each of us the courage to face whatever challenges the week might bring, and inspiring us with hope for a good, pleasant, and satisfying tomorrow.

*   *   *

While reminiscing about those scherished blessings, the heartfelt wishes, and the sage advice, I suddenly felt that I was hearing them again and I became very excited — it dawned on me how I could follow in my mother's footsteps! Recalling the words that I had heard in my mother's home over the decades could serve as a bridge to the past, and as a means to draw nearer to the good and the noble to which she guided me!

By "bridge," I mean, of course, a bridge of words. During her lifetime, my mother strung her pearls of wisdom on the twisting thread of life, pearl by pearl. She drew them out of the depths of wisdom and understanding, lovingly making them into a necklace for us.

This wonderful necklace was revealed to me section by section, brightly and graciously from all the family events in our home. It lent emphasis to that which had to be accented and blurred what needed to be erased. The necklace was fortified with links of pure fear of Heaven, and its pearls radiated the glow of love.

With great excitement, I began to string the necklace anew, rejoicing over each saying as it came to mind. I hurried to write them down on any available scrap of paper, even if it happened to be the back of a bus ticket or an envelope.

Gems kept popping up almost anywhere, causing even people around me to be amazed at the magnitude and quality of the treasure that I merited to inherit. Occasionally I had to stop in the middle of what I was doing, to write down a saying that had suddenly come to me. Once in a while I awakened from sleep to do the same. My notes were all over the house, and my family would gather them for me with a smile.

About six years after my mother's passing I had a collection of about 500 sayings, pertaining to all areas of life!

My mother did not bequeath any jewelry. She had left, in her parents' home in Europe, all the jewelry she had received in her youth, not wanting to make herself stand out in Eretz Yisrael, where such things were uncommon. She did leave a vast treasure of spiritual assets, however, chiseled out of eternal truths, and with everlasting radiance.

At first I used this treasure to try and give pleasure to people who were close to me, that is, my family and co-workers. After becoming convinced of their remarkable universal value, however, I decided to make them available to you as well, my dear readers.

MAY THESE WORDS BE A TESTIMONIAL
IN MEMORY OF
MY MOTHER, MY TEACHER
CHAYA FREIDA BAS RABBI YEHUDAH ARYEH LEIB, ע"ה